"You matter to me,
    simple and plain and ... from
                    somebody"

Wowie Chris! Where has the time gone?
From hearing you walk down the hall with
your electric toothbrush twice a day, to making
random last minute baked goods, to talks
about life and religion, to now, we've come a
long way. I am eternally grateful for your
friendship, Chris. You showed me that there is
always reason to smile and be goofy when
times get rough. You proved to me the value
in holding your ground, even when those around
you think differently. You pushed me to stay in
the game at NU, even when I felt like getting
out. I can't imagine my college experience
without you Chris. You helped me get through
one of the toughest battles I have ever had to
face with my eating, just by being there, and
for that I am forever indebted to you. Thank
you for the constant laughter and smiles.
I love and respect you to the moon and back.

This is one of my favorite acting books... you
might even say it's my acting bible. Maybe you
will find it to be as inspiring as I did. →

Regardless I hope it proves an interesting read. Congrats Chris! Can't wait to join you on this next big adventure.

"It's you I like" —Mr. Rogers

♡ Amy

How to Stop Acting

HOW TO
STOP ACTING

Harold Guskin

Farrar, Straus and Giroux
New York

Farrar, Straus and Giroux
18 West 18th Street, New York 10011

Copyright © 2003 by Harold Guskin and David Finkle
Introduction copyright © 2003 by Kevin Kline
Printed in the United States of America
First edition, 2003

Library of Congress Cataloging-in-Publication Data
Guskin, Harold, 1941–
    How to stop acting / Harold Guskin. — 1st ed.
        p.   cm.
    ISBN: 978-0-571-19999-0 (pbk. : alk. paper)
    1. Acting.   2. Acting—Psychological aspects.   I. Title.

PN2061 .G79 2003
792'.028—dc21

                                    2003040891

Designed by Abby Kagan

www.fsgbooks.com

19   21   23   22   20   18

For my wife, Sandra,
who taught me how to live

O, for a muse of fire that would ascend
The brightest heaven of invention

—William Shakespeare

I am certain of nothing but the
holiness of the heart's affections
and the truth of imagination—what
the imagination seizes as beauty
must be truth—whether it existed
before or not.

—John Keats,
letter to Benjamin Bailey,
22 November 1817

CONTENTS

INTRODUCTION

I have always felt indirectly responsible for Harold Guskin becoming an acting teacher. Harold was an actor and director and my fellow member in a theater company when we were in college. One day, he was leading me and two other actors through an improvisation. I was so bad that he stopped the exercise and more or less announced that he couldn't take it anymore. He told us that before he directed us in another play, he was going to teach us how to act.

We had been studying acting, reading our Stanislavski, observing the masters, performing in plays, and doing a pretty fair job of imitating what we thought acting looked and sounded like. But it wasn't the real thing, and we knew it. What Harold taught us was very complicated and very simple. He reconnected us to ourselves and painstakingly disconnected us from the time-honored hackneyed acting grammar in which we floundered and flailed. "Stop acting," he would say continually. I told Harold he should call his book *How to Stop Acting*.

Harold has the uncanny ability to guide actors through their rawest selves toward the most important and interesting truths through the text. The text is the source and the actor is the resource to the text. He taught us how to respond instinctively to the text but more importantly, to take personal responsibility for the text. A whole new world suddenly opened up for us. And all this was just on the first day.

I don't think anyone can teach a person how to act. I think ultimately we teach ourselves. But Harold gave me a compass with a *true* north, put me on a path, taught me how to navigate, and, best of all, taught me the sheer joy that acting can bring to those of us who are blessed and cursed enough to pursue it.

—Kevin Kline

PROLOGUE

I was twenty-five years old when I sneaked into my first acting class. I was finishing my studies at the Manhattan School of Music while performing professionally as a trombonist in symphony orchestras. But although I loved music, I didn't feel fulfilled. I found myself spending most of my time going to plays, both on and off Broadway. I was reading Stanislavski, and the plays of Anton Chekhov, Eugene O'Neill, Tennessee Williams, Arthur Miller, Samuel Beckett, and Jean Genet. Finally, I sneaked into this class.

When the teacher asked for someone to go on stage to do an improvisation, my hand flew up in the air. I volunteered so quickly because I was afraid that once I saw someone else on that stage, I would be too shy to go up. So up I went, with no real idea what an acting improvisation was.

I was to come in the door—a real door, upstage center. I was to do an improvisation that would tell the audience what the weather was outside.

For some reason, while I was backstage my imagination took off. I saw myself in the Irish countryside on a cold, stormy night. I was lost. There was a pub. In I came through the door. I shook the rain from my hat and coat. After a moment, I realized something was wrong. There was silence. I looked around the pub. Unfriendly men were looking at me. I smiled, walked to a table, sat down, and waited for someone to take my order. No one came. I didn't look up. I was chilled and afraid. I felt unwelcome, utterly alone. I waited. The silence seemed dangerous. Suddenly I slammed my fist on the table and yelled, "What the hell are you looking at!"

The class roared with laughter. I hadn't realized it was funny. But what surprised me most was that, while I had been aware that I was on stage the entire time, that awareness was not in the least distracting. My concentration was on this strange thing happening to me in the pub of my mind. My fantasy was as real to me as anything I had ever experienced. My feelings were totally free and bubbling up in me. It was a strong emotion to feel so isolated in that pub, or maybe on that stage. My instinct took me to this bold, unpredictable choice: to blow up and yell. I hadn't thought of doing that. It just happened.

It was thrilling. I felt alive. I thought to myself afterwards, This must be what it feels like when you're the soloist in the middle of the Tchaikovsky Violin Concerto and not the bass trombonist in the back of the orchestra. But it was a feeling I recognized from my trombone playing, too, when I was working with a great conductor and a great orchestra. I would let go of fear and trust myself completely. That was always when I did my best work, as if I were improvising on the notes of the music—even though, being a classically trained musician rather than a jazz player, I learned to do my improvisation on the notes given me, instead of making them up.

When I formally took up the study of acting, I learned more from the books I read than from any of my classes. I began, like almost everyone else in the 1960s, with Stanislavski. Then came Richard Boleslavsky's *The First Six Lessons*, Michael Chekhov's *The Actor at Work*, Viola Spolin's *Theater Games*, Michel Saint-Denis's *Theater: The Real Discovery of Style*, and books by Peter Brook, Antonin Artaud, and Jerzy Grotowsky. I explored their work and tried out their ideas for myself. Some of it seemed to work immediately. Some of it worked for a while and then became a problem, so I abandoned it. Some of it affected me only years later in my work on stage and in film. But all of it inspired me and gave me a framework for thinking about acting that I couldn't get as directly in class.

It was *An Actor Prepares*, though, that became my bible. I took every page, every exercise to heart. I became the "student" to whom Stanislavski continually refers in the book, the student striving to become an actor, the student guided by Stanislavski into the profound search for truth. I have to say that when I talk about Stanislavski, I'm still moved. It was a thrilling way to enter the world of theater, and I know it was my personal explorations with *An Actor Prepares* that gave me the confidence to test my wings.

When I started acting professionally, which was very soon after I began my studies, I approached my work on stage as Stanislavski outlines. I analyzed the script for the basic motivation of the character—what Stanislavski calls "the super-objective"—and for the character's "objective," the motivations or actions that propelled a scene's conflict. I wrote out my character's history at great length. I searched endlessly within myself for personal experiences to fill the character with emotion and practiced getting into my memories for use on stage when needed, via Stanislavski's technique of Emotion-Memory. I obsessed day and night about my character.

It all made sense. And at first my work impressed directors and audiences. I was active, energized, effective. But after a while, I found that when I was on stage, both in rehearsal and in performance, I wasn't as free as I knew I needed to be. I was not available in a fluid way to my feelings, to my imagination, to my instinct. I was not in the moment. And that was because I felt constrained by the techniques that were supposed to fill the scene with feeling. I was so diligently trying to "play my objective" that I was not free to do anything else on stage. I was not in a genuine state of exploration, so my acting was not surprising, to me or to the audience. I was too neat, too logical. My characters lacked the amazing variety of life.

Feeling this way—not free but obligated, uninspired, out of touch with my feelings, instinct, and imagination—I eventually recalled that first improvisation of mine. That's when I gave up thinking about acting strictly according to Stanislavski's dictates, specifically the analysis. Instead of beginning my work on the character by analyzing the script scene by scene, I started improvising on the lines moment by moment. And I did this without—and this is crucial—ever changing any of the lines. It was as if I were a trombonist again, improvising on my part without taking liberties with any of the notes.

I took the risk of simply responding to my line and the other characters' lines without regard for anything but what I felt at the moment, what interested me right then. I explored the text on my feet in rehearsal, and kept on exploring in performance. I let go of technique and analysis. My exploration, moment by moment, became the character.

This allowed me to feel free, and it led to a much more interesting character as well as a more creative solution to the problem of a given scene—precisely, I believe, because I was forced to rely only on myself and the text. There was no analysis of the scene to obligate me or to protect me, and therefore my instincts surfaced with energy and vigor. The character came alive, because I was already inside him.

The character *was* me at that moment. I was therefore free to do whatever was provoked by the lines of dialogue. Yet my responses and choices were quite different from my usual choices in life. They surprised me, just as my responses had in the pub improvisation. I was, and still am, very shy in front of people I don't know, and I am quiet much of the time. But I found myself responding to the character's lines quite easily, in uncharacteristic, unplanned ways. My responses struck me as arbitrary, yet somehow at the same time connected by the lines of the text to the character.

The lines were bouncing off parts of me I hadn't used much—in fact, parts I didn't even know existed. But line by line, response by response, moment by moment, they *were* me. Strung together by the text, though, they didn't look or feel like me to anyone else. Only to me. And so I began to arrive at characters who were different from each other and from me, yet paradoxically were totally me.

The most surprising thing of all was that it was easy. So much so that I could see why actors might distrust it. Art is supposed to be hard, isn't it? The more blood we let in the process of dissecting our psyches, the better the performance, right? Maybe not! Ease not only releases us as actors, it releases the audience as well, simply to look and listen and forget that they are watching acting. They're spared the strain of it all. They don't know what they're going to see, so they have to follow. It all becomes as surprising to them as it is for us. We are all now in the same moment.

The only thing that was hard was to have the courage not to give a damn what came out, or what came next, or how unexpected the choice was. If I didn't know, or for that matter care, where I was going moment by moment, I was more available to the text in a creative way. I remember being on stage in performance, so fully in the moment that I had no idea what the next line was. And when the moment arrived, I would take a breath and let it come to me. It always did. I'd find myself enraged at one moment, shouting the line, then the next line would come to me as delicate, loving. Instead of barreling through the script, keeping the wild modulations at bay, or doubting myself and ignoring where the impulse wanted to take me, I would take a breath, exhale, and simply let the next line come in and take me on a trip to a new place. Other actors would compliment me on my transitions, but all I was really doing was responding to each line—to each moment. It took guts not to try to control anything—to let myself go with whatever came to me or whatever interested me. It also took courage to forget about time, to take it at my own pace, being patient enough to let the lines in and see how they worked on me just then—or sometimes, to leap on a response before I had a chance to censor it.

I began to understand that to find the most interesting character he has within him, the actor has to be open to the cheapest as well as the deepest things that play on him. He can't censor anything, including what may seem like inappropriate choices. And because the actor doesn't know whether a feeling is right until it comes out, he must get it out before he has a chance to choose. He must leave it to his instinct. I'm not saying that any stupid choice is going to be all right in the end. But if he doesn't get that stupid choice out at the beginning, he will not get beyond it to the good stuff. And if a seemingly inappropriate choice works, it may be better than good. It may be great!

There are a lot of ways to teach acting. Before Stanislavski, it was only about voice, body, and speech training. Then Stanislavski gave us a "system" of acting based on the psychology of the character and ideas of how to use oneself and one's memories to define character. Since then, there have been many variations on Stanislavski's system. They have all, however, been modeled in one way or another after his basic precepts—his Method. And they are all about How to Act.

My debt to Stanislavski and the many other great acting teachers I discovered in my early reading is enormous. But any theory or analysis puts the actor in his mind, not his instinct. Once the actor feels an obligation to fulfill and justify a choice, he is not free to go anywhere else. He can no longer explore. He becomes aware of what he's going to do and how he's going to do it. As a result, his instinct shuts down. This is because, for all of us, anything instinctive feels dangerous. We can't control it. Therefore the mind, reacting to danger, will often reject instinct and opt for the safe, thought-out choice. But this leaves the actor no longer on the edge. And no matter how gifted he is, he will betray his safe choice to the audience, to the camera, and to himself. The surprise, the life, will be gone from stage or film.

Many actors fear that an instinctive approach leads to characters that are just the actor. As I discovered, the text takes care of that. Every script is different, and if the actor is truly responding without limitations to the text, each character will affect the actor in a different way. His instinct and imagination will take him to places unlike himself or his image of himself, even though they are all, moment by moment, him.

Character is not some painted-on picture of what the actor or director thinks the character should be. The character is a real person. And so I as an actor must be real—I must be completely personal, so that the audience see a real, breathing human in front of them. My personal response to the text may be called an interpretation by critics and the audience after they see it. But for me, it is simply my response to the dialogue and action. That's why it is believable as well as creative.

My approach is to give up the idea of acting for what I think of as simply allowing oneself to respond to the text. Instead of yet another method, I offer a strategy based on a radically simple idea: that the actor's work is not to create a character but to be continually, personally responsive to the text, wherever his impulse takes him, from first read-through to final performance. If the actor trusts that, he will be transformed into the character through the text.

For me, acting is a constantly evolving exploration rather than a progression toward a fixed goal. The character emerges in response to the text as long as the actor is in a state of exploration with it, line by line, every moment. And in order to do this one has to let go of technique, control, propriety, preconceived notions, obligations, and, most difficult, the fear of being foolish, and the fear that you won't find the character if you work this way.

This book is about letting yourself become the character, and about a way not to Act. It's about how to throw away technique so that instinct can surface. It's about a transformation into the character that happens with ease, and with nothing to rely on but oneself and the text. I offer the actor a way to immerse himself in the script as quickly and easily as possible, to establish a direct connection between himself and the material. This exploration, moment by moment, begun alone and then continued through rehearsal and into performance on stage or before the camera, becomes the character.

Because of the nontheoretical nature of my strategy, when I was asked to write a book about what I do, I wasn't sure it would be possible.

I had plenty of experience to draw on, of course. I had been coaching actors for more than thirty years, ever since I was an artist in residence at Indiana University, where I acted with the Indiana Theater Company, a classical repertory ensemble. At the time, there was a small company of undergraduates performing improvisations at a coffeehouse known as The Owl. They called themselves the Vest Pocket Players, and Kevin Kline was one of them.

My memory of what happened differs slightly from Kevin's. I think these young actors asked for my help because they recognized a freedom in my acting. While I was clearly serious about it, I wasn't afraid to do outrageous things on stage. I was willing to accept bits and pieces of the many approaches to acting as long as they worked for me, but I trusted my instinct to guide me, whereas these younger actors felt hampered by what they thought they were supposed to do and were tied in knots by the struggle.

I hadn't planned on teaching, but I told Kevin and the group that if they shut up long enough for me to figure out what I was doing, I would be glad to start a small class. Shortly after I began the class, Kevin was given his first leading role in a main stage production at the university, and I began to work one-on-one with him, coaching him for the part.

"You took me line by line through the scenes," Kevin recalls. "I remember you reading with me and saying, 'What does this line mean to you?' I thought, Who cares what it means to me? What's the right way to say it? Up until that point, I would look at a line and say, 'How would Olivier or Brando deliver it?' Just as I assumed a painter would say, 'How would Velázquez paint this?' or a musician would say, 'How would Horowitz play this?' But you said, 'When you are on stage, if it's going to be alive, as opposed to some idea you are showing us or indicating to us about this character, you have to take responsibility for that line. So tell me what that line means to you.' "

As Kevin progressed through the script, he began to allow himself to stop interpreting the character intellectually and to simply respond to the words, phrases, and lines personally, so they meant something to him. "This huge gaping door opened to me," Kevin says. "At the risk of sounding pretentious, I suddenly realized that this is what being an interpretive artist is. I actually bring something to bear on this material. Me!"

We talked about what each line meant to Kevin, and also what the play as a whole meant to him personally. "It was thrilling," he remembers. "Where I once would have written 'ideas' in the margin of a script, I now found myself writing over and over again, *Trust yourself, trust yourself*."

Kevin's acting began to become totally instinctive in a personal way that would evolve into his signature style. He played his role in the university production with an individuality that made people take notice of him. He was unpredictable, and therefore fun to watch. Important roles started to come his way. With each role, he explored different aspects of himself. His range increased as he allowed himself to be genuinely stimulated by the different texts he tackled and the characters within them.

This was the beginning of our exploration together, and it continues to the present—this process of immersion in the script, in the dialogue, so that the character is completely personal, believable, and unpredictable. From that fortuitous encounter with Kevin, I began to work with other actors, and coaching took on the shape of a vocation, along with my continued work as an actor, director, and teacher.

I found I particularly liked coaching because I could tailor the teaching to the individual actor and help him deal with his specific problems in an immediate way. I could sit across from him and respond to what he was doing at that exact moment. I could watch and listen and make no judgments. I could abandon theory for a hands-on, personal approach, helping each actor to find his own way as I had found mine.

When I decided to write a book, however, I wasn't sure I could translate what actors do with me in the privacy of the studio onto the page. To find out, I enlisted the aid of a knowledgeable theater writer, David Finkle, and a number of my clients—in addition to Kevin, Glenn Close, James Gandolfini, Matt Dillon, Christopher Reeve, Peter Fonda, Bridget Fonda, Ally Sheedy, Jennifer Jason Leigh, Tcheky Karyo, Chris Noth, and several others—with whom I could review our collaborative work. When they talked about what I'd done with them, I was surprised to see that it followed a distinct, graspable, and consistent pattern. Without trying to, it seemed I'd developed an "approach."

The actors' take on what I do has been invaluable, and I have therefore incorporated it throughout this book, often in their own pertinent and persuasive words. I've included as well the solutions they've found to the real challenges of acting professionally on stage, in films, and on television. But above all, the book is about what I did and what I do to help actors feel free, creative, and truthful, to help the actor allow instinct, emotion, and the rawness of real life to emerge within him to become the character. And this is all so the actor does not have to Act the character.

My hope for this book is that it will offer actors what the acting texts I studied offered me—a window into myself and a source of personal power and emotion. Do with it what you will. Use parts of it, or none of it, or all of it. If it gets you to think about acting from another point of view, my effort in writing it will have been well spent.

How to Stop Acting

1

TAKING IT OFF THE PAGE

"I'm basically a shy person, and I can get as shy in front of a character that I have been hired to inhabit as I can in front of an actual breathing human being. A lot of what we worked on when we first got together was getting through my shyness in relationship to the character whose words had to come out of my mouth."

—Glenn Close

Actors come to me for all sorts of reasons, at every stage of their careers. Matt Dillon came to me for the first time with a stack of research he'd done for his role in *Drugstore Cowboy*. Christopher Reeve came at a low point, showing the courage to rediscover himself in his work. James Gandolfini continued to examine Tony Soprano with me in *The Sopranos'* second and third seasons, after a hugely successful first year. Glenn Close came because of a problem with auditioning. Glenn says:

You have to force yourself to get through that barrier of shyness—to force the words out, to speak them—so you can slowly start getting beyond that and into the character. That kind of training has stood me in great stead. You find yourself on a movie set doing a scene and you know you're not there. At that moment, I have learned to say, "Don't lose courage. Just keep leaping out there. Be able to make a fool of yourself." And because you've not gotten frightened, and you haven't retreated from the moment, if you persevere, you'll find it. I think those early days of me sitting in your living room and forcing myself to say words that I had no idea how to say—getting them out, flinging them out, throwing them out—was like breaking some sort of sound barrier, giving me freedom on the other side.

In the conventional view, the actor's work on the character begins with his reading the script for himself and then talking about the character and text with the director. The problem with this approach is that from the beginning of the process it places the actor outside the script, and outside the character. And being outside the script and the character means that the actor is fundamentally *outside himself*—outside of the instinct, feelings, imagination, and fantasy life necessary to conceive the character creatively. He may arrive at an extremely sophisticated understanding of the character that nevertheless leaves him utterly confused about how to put his analysis into action.

That is because reading the script is an intellectual process that inevitably leads the actor to approach both character and script as we have been taught in school—in an analytical way. Whether it's Stanislavskian analysis or some sort of literary analysis, it leads the actor to *think* about the character rather than instinctively to try out different possibilities for the character. In fact, analysis tends to make the actor afraid of trusting his instinct. It leads to doubts about whether his mind is crisp enough to grasp quickly enough the character's central needs in life or his desires in a particular scene, as Stanislavski instructs. Analysis weakens the actor.

Glenn Close, one of the most intelligent actors I know, told me, "I don't pride myself on being able to read a script really well.

There are some people who can sit down and really analyze it and get its full value immediately, but it takes me a while." Analysis is not really what actors are good at, although most really good actors are quite smart. It should be left to literary scholars and critics. Actors are about feelings, imagination, and improvisation. They are good at becoming other people. Their instinct is their talent. The more they trust their instinct, the more inspired and inspiring their performances become. That is when they surprise us, even startle us. That is what the audience goes to see.

It's not that intellect is unimportant. It's just not where the actor's work starts. *I believe that it's not until the actor is actually verbalizing the words of the character that his real work in acting begins.* No matter how experienced or inexperienced he is, the most important thing for him to do is to connect himself to the text—to the dialogue, to the words. At that moment, he has connected himself to the character in a real way—even a physical way, as the words come out of his mouth. If he is able truly to speak the character's dialogue, rather than to read or recite it, he is in fact inside the character's head. He will feel free with the dialogue and the choices it provokes. His fear of finding the character will diminish. If he can be in the moment, in the script, and in himself at the same time—floating with the line—his instincts and the script will take him where he needs to go. If the actor can connect in a personal and instinctive way to the words his character speaks, moment by moment, at the very outset of his work, then he will begin his exploration from *within the character.*

The actor has to start from his visceral response to the material. This is why he must reject intellectual choices at the beginning of his work. He must allow himself to be in an exploratory state, unsure of what he is going to do; this forces him to trust his initial responses to the dialogue, regardless of how absurd or contrary they may seem. If he is analytical, his intellect will stifle these reactions.

But the moment when the words must come out of the actor's mouth is always the most fearful, as Glenn Close so vividly describes. It's the ultimate showdown. And because it is so daunting, the actor does what he can to avoid or postpone it, even when he says the words aloud. Each time he picks up a new script and starts to read it out loud, he is tempted to "make it real." By *real*, he inevitably means conversational or natural or casual. If the actor is a quick study and what is considered in the business a "good reader," he will make the dialogue sound as if it's real even while he has his nose buried in the text. That seems like the smart thing to do.

The problem is, it's a useless thing to do because the actor is approximating, no matter how deftly, a realistic line reading—that is, how the dialogue *might* go. And in the process, he is establishing rhythms and choices he doesn't even know he wants. He's imitating the way he thinks it *should* go, and before long he may find himself stuck in those line readings and those choices without being aware of it. At best, he'll have to break the pattern in order to feel free and to find fresh responses, real responses.

When an actor comes to work with me, I want real, fresh responses from the beginning. So whether he's a seasoned actor taking on his umpteenth major role, or a young actor just starting out, we begin the same way. We go back to the barre, like a ballet dancer, starting from zero with a simple but effective exercise that allows the actor to discover or rediscover the foundation of acting through the text, with no preconceptions of how to play the role. I call this process *taking it off the page*.

Here's how it works: The actor looks down at the phrase and breathes in and out while he reads the words to himself, giving himself time to let the phrase into his head. Then he looks up from the page and says the line, no longer reading but speaking.

Taking your time to breathe in and out while you look down at the page to read the phrase for yourself allows you to access whatever unconscious thoughts or images it evokes. It doesn't matter what comes up—however trivial, simple, deep, or apparently unrelated it is—as long as it is your actual response at the time, and not what you *think* is appropriate.

The point is to let the dialogue bounce around in your unconscious, a bit like in the Freudian concept of word association in which the psychoanalyst says a word and the patient responds with whatever word comes to mind, before he can censor it. The actor is accessing his unconscious self, surprising himself with his unconscious response, in much the same way.

As soon as you exhale, say the phrase before you have a chance to censor whatever thought or feeling surfaces. Don't deaden the line by trying to be sincere. Just say what you mean, no matter how startling, stupid, frightening, funny, touching, irreverent, or boring. Exhaling before you speak ensures that it is your own voice that you are using, not a phony, artificially projected actor's voice. It is the way we all speak when we are not acting.

Once the feeling has surfaced and been expressed, feel free to drop it so that the next line can take you to a new place. Actors often hold on to a feeling or thought that's working, out of fear that they'll have nothing else to replace it that will be as good. But the truth is, holding on to the thought or feeling evoked by one line limits the possible range of responses the next line can elicit; letting go leaves room for something new to arise. That's what exploration is all about.

Often actors are afraid they won't have a feeling for the writer's line. And sometimes the honest response to a line is, I don't feel or think anything. If so, that's what you must say—with the writer's words. Surprisingly, that response is as good and useful as any other. That's because it is a truthful response. In real life, we often don't know what we feel or think, or whether we have a response at all. It takes courage to admit to yourself that you don't really have any feelings about something. Even more courage is needed to avoid manufacturing a false feeling to please those around you.

This admission is not only important, it's essential! *Nothing* is powerful when admitted in front of an audience or a camera. Doing nothing puts the audience on notice that the person in front of us is real. I am not manufacturing feelings and thoughts because it's expected of me, he is saying. His *no-response* makes him more dangerous, unsocialized, surprising. We don't know what he may do next. This makes the actor interesting.

One of the reasons people love James Gandolfini's portrayal of Tony Soprano is that it's filled with a lot of unusual responses and unexpected choices. People often assume this comes from a process of breaking down the script and selecting from among his responses in advance. But in fact, when I work with Jim, often the most important thing he does is to admit that he doesn't know what he feels about a scene or a moment. By accepting this and allowing himself to do nothing, he is making himself available to the surprising and unpredictable responses that follow.

The beginning actor will also discover that if he has no feeling one moment, he will find himself angry or frustrated or saddened or amused the next moment. And it will probably be a big feeling.

An actor doing nothing is doing a great deal. Think of the end of *The Grapes of Wrath*. Ma Joad asks Tom, "But Tommy—how will I know where you are?" And Henry Fonda (as Tom) answers, "Wherever there are cops beating on fellas, I'll be there, Ma . . . "

Recalling this classic moment, Peter Fonda told me, "My father stayed with his Nebraska cadence. He hardly blinked and he just read the words as simple and flat and straight as it could be. Thinking back on it, had he put any dramatic spin on it, facial or verbal or tonal, those words would have been the corniest words in the world."

Doing this—doing nothing—allowed the truth of that moment to emerge powerfully.

Don't get too exacting about how much text to take off the page at a time. You may pick up a phrase or a whole line or even a couple of short lines at once. Do whatever your instinct tells you, or choose arbitrarily. In fact, breaking the normal rhythms of your speech can make you more open to characters with different, new, and unexpected rhythms. But what matters most is that you say what you mean, whatever that is.

Most important of all, *don't be careful!* These are your lines, your images, your thoughts. Don't think of taking it off the page as a technique so much as a commonsense way to start your work. The exploration you are beginning is going to become the character. Because you are within the script, anything you do could be or could become the character. You are in a state of discovery triggered by the only thing we know for sure about the character— what the character says. This leaves you free to try anything that comes to you.

Let me show you how taking it off the page works in practice. Suppose I am starting my work on Michael Weller's play *Loose Ends*, in the role of Paul. The play opens with the monologue on the following page.

The first line is, "It was great at the beginning." I look down at the page and read the line to myself while taking a breath in and out. At another time, or for another actor, it might conjure up, say, the beginning of a relationship that has since broken up, but right now it evokes in me the memory of directing my first play as a graduate student, with Kevin Kline and the Vest Pocket Players. We were so young and everything was ahead of us. I look up from the page and say the line, relishing the memory.

If I trust myself, I won't have to do anything but say the line, and my response will be visible. I won't have to add anything. No

From *Loose Ends* by Michael Weller (*Five Plays*. New York: New American Library, 1982.)

SCENE 1

Slide: 1970. A beach. Night. Full moon. Waves. On bare stage, Paul and Susan, early to mid-20's, naked, clothes around. He sits facing ocean (us) and she lies curled up.

PAUL. It was great at the beginning. I could speak the language almost fluently after a month and the people were fantastic. They'd come out and help us. Teach us songs. Man, we thought it was all going so well. But we got all the outhouses dug in six months and we had to stay there two years, that was the deal. And that's when we began to realize that none of the Nglele were using the outhouses. We'd ask them why and they'd just shrug. So we started watching them very carefully and what we found out was the Nglele use their feces for fertilizer. It's like gold to them. They thought we were all fucking crazy expecting them to waste their precious turds in our spiffy new outhouses. Turns out they'd been helping us because they misunderstood why we were there. They thought it was some kind of punishment and we'd be allowed to go home after we finished digging the latrines, that's why they were helping us and then when we stayed on they figured we must be permanent outcasts or something and they just stopped talking to us altogether.

one will know the specifics of what I'm thinking, because I say only the line Weller wrote. But if I trust myself to *just say it*, the line will be full. Most actors don't trust themselves to just say it, however. They don't trust that what they are thinking or feeling is enough. They want to *do something* with the line. They want to show us their thought or feeling.

I want the actor to say what he means at that moment, with as little fuss as possible. He must let the line of the character become his own line, in a completely personal way, so he is not acting it.

He must forget about the author's intention at first, because the actor doesn't know who the character is at this point, or what the author really wants. The actor is responsible only for what the line means to him right now, and what it creates in him. And so he must say only what he means, without embellishing it or fixing it up.

I look down and take another breath in and out while reading the next phrase: "I could speak the language almost fluently." I don't force myself to read the whole line. I let in whatever is comfortable, sometimes only a phrase or even a word. I think, It would be nice to be fluent in another language, especially since I love to travel. I look up and say what I mean, without fussing with it.

Looking down, I find the next part of the line—"after a month." As I breathe in and out I think, Wow—only a month! I look up, and that's what I say with the phrase.

The rest of the line is "and the people were fantastic." Looking down at the line, I have an image of friendly natives in a remote part of Africa or the Amazon. I haven't been to those places but it doesn't matter, because my imagination takes over. "They'd come out and help us. Teach us songs." As I read this to myself while breathing, this image becomes so vivid in my imagination that I have the desire to sing some sort of work song. So before I can censor this desire, I improvise a little song and dance. Then I say the line. It is silly and foolish, but it makes me happy, and strangely enough, it doesn't really feel wrong after I do it. What seemed like it might be inappropriate didn't feel that way when I did it. It was my response to the line—to the image. And the line is the character's. So maybe this *is* the character.

When I'm taking the lines off the page, I trust myself to respond to whatever comes to me. An hour later, or even a few minutes later, I might have the opposite response. But I can't let myself be judgmental. Letting the line become mine means I don't need to justify what I do. I let the words, thoughts, and images stimulate me so that I lose myself in the lines. My imagination takes over, and I am connected to the words of the writer viscerally, not intellectually.

I look down, laughing, and continue: "Man, we thought it was all going so well." As I let the line into myself while breathing in and out, I feel a disappointment in the line come over me. I let the change take me, and I say it.

The twists and turns in the feelings that the lines generate are interesting and energizing. Looking down at the page, I read, "But we got all the outhouses dug in six months." Outhouses?! This is incredible, I think. "And we had to stay there two years, that was the deal." I see this on the page. I breathe in and out, thinking, We're screwed. No one in his right mind could have expected to be digging outhouses when we signed on. I feel stupid. I am reminded of many choices I made in my career without really knowing the deal or the consequences. But instead of feeding my anger, the next line—"And that's when we began to realize that none of the Nglele were using these outhouses"—confuses me. Breathing in and out, I let this confusion take me to "We asked them why and they'd just shrug." The next line—"So we started watching them very carefully"—gets me interested. As I breathe in and out, I see myself in a remote area, hiding behind latrines, sneaking around trees to spy on the Nglele. I look down and pick up the next line while breathing in and out—"What we found was the Nglele use their feces for fertilizer." This sets me to imagining what it would be like to cherish one's feces. I read, "It's like gold to them," and as I breathe out, I am prompted to sniff the imagined gold feces that I now have in my hands, as if sniffing a delicate flower. It's idiotic, I know. But I'm feeling idiotic. And because I'm free, I do it. I know that if it's no good, I won't do it again next time, because I will have gotten that response out of my system.

But I need to express my feelings as they arise, to get each one out before I censor it. I have to trust my outrageous responses as much as the subtle ones.

That's what taking it off the page is about—being free to let the phrase or line take me wherever it goes at that moment. I do this before I know anything much. I have read the play. But this is my first real reading of the play out loud, the beginning of my work on the character. So making mistakes, doing stupid, outrageous things, and simply exploring my responses to the text are not only acceptable but also necessary steps. The more I get out at the beginning, the less careful I am, the bigger my palette, the more possibilities for the character later on. I would rather find myself throwing away choices because I have too many than have to struggle to find enough colors for the character.

When I recently asked Jennifer Jason Leigh about our work together on *Miami Blues*, she said, "I like the way you explore things. There's something very gentle about it that allowed me to be myself within the part and create a character at the same time. The way you would have me breathe into a line, just stay inside the breath, and let the thoughts come. Not forcing yourself to think anything. Not forcing yourself to figure out what your objective was or anything else. But just stay[ing] inside the moment and see[ing] what that brings."

What the process revealed to her "was a tremendous amount of life and things that I wouldn't necessarily have thought. Because it wasn't about a thought process." By just living inside the character, "just breathing and allowing your mind and your body to free associate—within the confines of the material—you'll surprise yourself in a way that's really lovely and feels organic."

It's easy for an actor to think he is past this initial step, but he never is. Even highly experienced actors struggle with the beginning of their work. I have to remind them to be patient, to let the line come to them before they say it, to make sure it is theirs. Glenn Close says that after all these years, she still begins her work on new characters by taking it off the page. "I tend to go too fast," she says. "What that does is force me to go slower. You can find moments. You have to give yourself time."

Christopher Reeve is an actor for whom establishing an immediate connection to the text became the key to a radically different way of approaching acting. Chris had become a big star very early. He came to me when his career had begun to fizzle a bit. He recalls, "I was always employable but never really, really nailed it, probably because I had so much success so early—first Broadway with Katharine Hepburn, then *Superman*, and then on to big roles in movies. Unfortunately, what happens if you're the star and they're paying you a ton of money is they stop directing. They think, Well, he knows what he's doing—he's a big star. And that's really, really dangerous. I was good enough to get away with it and get the next job. But I still had that problem of not really being in the moment."

When we began to work together, Chris remembers, "The first job was to get rid of a kind of analytical sense, intellectualization—my habit of approaching a scene as though I was doing a paper for college. I had to make room for something that might be more interesting."

> We'd sit there and read back and forth, simply listening and then looking down to see what the line is, and then, without thinking, responding. We got rid of any idea of how it ought to go. We worked on being inappropriate sometimes, just to bend things out of shape, because I'd come in with all my ducks lined up in a row—everything organized and a lot of ideas about how it should be.
>
> I'd read, and you'd stop me every time I was doing something

that had a plan to it, that was "appropriate," that didn't just happen immediately and spontaneously, that didn't just come in the moment. The best piece of advice—the mantra for me—became "I don't care." It is an oddly backwards approach that I learned you need to take. If they would give out Oscars for being on time, knowing the words cold, and never missing a mark, I'd clean up. And what you always said was, "Look, you have got to do what you are going to do and they have to find you." So in other words, what might seem in me like carelessness—"I don't care"—really was the beginning of freedom. "I don't care, I don't know what's going to happen, and I don't know what's going to come out of me—I'm just not going to worry about it." This was a major breakthrough from being sort of a good boy into being more reckless, more in the moment, and more daring in my acting. Not caring how it comes out creates moments that actually work. It's like when you step on a garden hose and then you release it and the water flows again. That's really what needed to happen to me. Because I had plenty of stuff to bring, but there was a kind of blockage because of this sense of responsibility, and my work wasn't flowing.

I believe the actor's relationship to what he says—his dialogue, his words—is the most important connection he makes. The text unearths previously hidden places within the actor, giving him a broader range of choices and characters, stimulated by the texts of many different and brilliant writers. It teaches the actor to see acting as *exploration of the character rather than definition of the character.*

Here's how the process might begin with a less experienced actor. Ellen Wolf has been studying with me for a couple of years, following a good deal of acting training. She is very talented, full of emotion and energy. She has a very good mind but sometimes uses it to cover herself. Her instincts and imagination are readily available to her, but she sometimes rushes because she's afraid to trust her responses. Her problem has always been a desire to act too much.

I hand Ellen a copy of Chekhov's *The Cherry Orchard* and point out a monologue in Act III. "You're too young for this part," I say, "but let's try it." I know she doesn't know anything about the character, Ranevskaya, or the monologue. She hasn't even read the play. This is a deliberate choice on my part. For the moment, I want her to have nothing to hold on to but the dialogue, no preconceived ideas about the character or the situation. I want her not to act, but simply to respond to what she sees, thinks, and says. I want her palette clean so that this response is her own, and immediate. I want to throw her into a confrontation with herself—to get her to trust herself. And I want her to get used to beginning this way.

From *The Cherry Orchard* by Anton Chekhov. (*Chekhov: The Major Plays*. Translation by Ann Dunnigan, New York: Signet Classics, 1964.)

ACT II

RANEVSKAYA. Oh, my sins . . . I've always squandered money recklessly, like a madwoman, and I married a man who did nothing but amass debts. My husband died from champagne—he drank terribly—then, to my sorrow, I fell in love with another man, lived with him, and just at that time—that was my first punishment, a blow on the head—my little boy was drowned . . . here in the river. And I went abroad, went away for good, never to return, never to see this river . . . I closed my eyes and ran, beside myself, and he after me . . . callously, without pity.

Ellen looks down at the page, takes a breath, looks up, and says simply, "Oh, my sins." Then she quickly looks down, takes a breath, looks up, and says, "I've always squandered money recklessly." She repeats the process with a couple more lines, each time too quickly.

I stop her. "Wait a minute. What's the first phrase?"

"Oh, my sins," she answers flatly.

"What?" I ask.

"My sins," she says.

"What do you mean?"

"My transgressions, the bad things I've done."

"Transgressions?" I repeat, disbelieving, as if the word were from a foreign language. What could such a word really mean to Ellen? She's in her head.

"My sins," she yells, as if talking to a deaf person. "What I've done badly."

"Anything come to mind?" I ask.

"Yes," she replies, laughing.

"So is that what you mean?"

"My sins, yeah," she answers simply, no longer laughing. She is getting closer to the word but she isn't there yet.

"So if I said, 'Why don't you tell me some of your sins? Would you be pleased to do that?' "

"No," she says, uncomfortably, "I doubt it."

"Right," I say pointedly.

And as if a light has turned on, she exclaims, "Oh!" And mumbles quietly, as if to herself, "Oh, my sins." A long pause follows. Then she looks down, breathes in and out, looks up slowly and says, almost as a confession, "I've always squandered money"—pause—"recklessly . . . "

She looks down, breathes in and out, looks up and says, "Like a madwoman."

"What do you mean?" I ask.

"Well," she says, "Just like overdoing things, buying things that I don't really need."

"Like what?" I ask.

"Large exercise equipment . . . Like a madwoman," she says, disgusted with herself.

"Stuff you don't need?" I ask.

"Yeah, insane stuff," she says angrily.

"Breathe," I remind her.

"And—"

"No, breathe before you talk."

She breathes out. "And I married a man," she says, "who did nothing—" She stops.

"Release," I prompt.

"—but amass debts," she goes on, still disgusted with herself.

"Just breathe and let it out."

"My husband died from champagne."

"Wait a second, what?" I ask.

"My husband died from champagne. He drank."

"What did he drink?" I ask.

"Champagne," she says, laughing—a whole new feeling has popped up in her. It makes me laugh.

"He drank, terribly," she goes on. "Then, to my sorrow."

"Breathe," I coach.

She looks down at the page. She seems confused as she breathes. "I fell in love with another man. Lived with him." She looks down, breathing in and out, then looks up and says, "And just at that time—[*louder*] that was my first punishment."

I stop her because she seems to be rushing again. "What is that line?"

"That was my first punishment."

"What are you saying?"

She takes a moment, then says, "That was the first time I got caught."

"That's what it means to you?" I ask.

"Yeah."

"So that's what you say."

"That was my first punishment," she says, now meaning it.

"Wait until it means whatever it means to you," I say. "That doesn't mean I want it soaked with emotion. You want to get inside the material so that you take responsibility for the line. For whatever it means to you. It's okay if it's not what Chekhov means. You'll figure it out at some point. The two of us know you haven't read this. You don't know anything about it. It's all a big surprise to you. Okay? So, no cover . . . no cover . . . no cover."

"Gotcha."

"The whole thing is just to take your chances," I go on. "You breathe, you look down, you let it in, and you say whatever it really means to you at the moment, including nothing. But also including—"

"Something."

"Right," I say, grinning. "Champagne? If what it means to you is, 'Hey, he died from champagne. He died good,' then great!" I sniff an imaginary glass. "Mmmmm, champagne. I think I'll go that way. If it means that, that's what it means, no matter how stupid or trivial. Maybe it is deep, like when you said, 'Like a madwoman.' You knew exactly what you meant—buying that stuff you don't want, but you've got to have it."

"Got it," Ellen says.

"Breathe. Next line, piece by piece."

There is a long pause, as Ellen breathes in and out. "A blow on the head," she says, and all of a sudden she starts to cry. "My little boy was drowned . . . here in the river." She tries to stop crying but can't, as she says the next lines. "Then I went abroad, went away for good. Never to return, never to see this river. I closed my eyes."

"What did you do?"

"I closed my eyes . . . I just closed my eyes . . . and ran." This line comes out with real power. When she says "and ran," I can feel her desperately wanting to run away.

We continue through the monologue together. Once Ellen stops rushing and lets the phrases and lines into herself, her emotions come leaping out. She goes all over the place while exploring Ranevskaya's lines, because she is totally in tune with herself. There are moments when she loses herself and weeps. At times she is angry. At other times she laughs at herself, at her foolishness. Occasionally she disagrees with a line and is angry at having to say it. So she speaks the line with her annoyance. The next time she says the line, or after she reads the play, she may no longer have that feeling, but for the time being she must accept it and express it, twisting and turning with whatever the text provokes in her.

Let's look at the process of taking it off the page with a scene. How does it work?

Suppose an actress, we'll call her Sophie, comes to me for help with the role of Masha in Chekhov's *The Seagull*. She has read the script. We begin our exploration together with the first scene of the play, which is between Masha and Medvedenko, the schoolteacher. (See box on opposite page.)

Typically, when actors are preparing for a first reading of a scene in a play or screenplay, they read the script for themselves many times. During this period on their own they make lots of decisions about the character. When they read out loud together for the first time, they invariably keep their noses in the text while they say their lines back and forth, each of them approximating "expressive" line readings. It is impossible for them to have actual responses because they are reading and are not available to one another, themselves, or the script.

I want the actor to come to a first reading with no decisions about the character. I want the first reading to be an open, no-holds-barred exploration that will allow the actor to start the process of discovering his character and himself within the script. I want him to simply take the lines off the page, connecting personally with his lines and listening to the other characters' lines without reading them as the other actors speak. In order to listen, the actor must not be looking at another actor's lines. His head cannot be in the page.

From *The Seagull* by Anton Chekhov. (*Chekhov: The Major Plays.* Translation by Ann Dunnigan. New York: Signet Classics, 1964.)

MEDVEDENKO. Why do you always wear black?

MASHA. I am in mourning for my life. I am unhappy.

MEDVEDENKO. Why? I don't understand . . . You are in good health, and your father, though not rich, is well off. My life is much harder than yours. I get only twenty-three rubles a month, and out of that they take something for the pension fund, but I don't wear mourning.

MASHA. It isn't a question of money. Even a beggar can be happy.

MEDVEDENKO. Yes, in theory, but in practice it's like this. There's me, my mother, my two sisters, and a little brother—on a salary of only twenty-three rubles. People have to eat and drink, don't they? And they need tea and sugar? And tobacco? It's not easy to make ends meet.

Since I'm reading Medvedenko, I have the first line. "Why do you always wear black?" Breathing in and out, I look up and ask the question simply.

Sophie can look at me or not, but she should not be reading

my line as I say it or as I read it for myself. Nor should she be reading ahead to see what her own next line is. If Sophie is reading, she can't really be listening, and if she isn't listening, she can't really respond. Without her response, her line will mean nothing. Listening is crucial to having a real response.

Maybe as Sophie listens, she's thinking, It's none of his business, or Who knows why I always wear black? Then, looking down at Masha's first line, "I'm in mourning for my life," she breathes in and out, thinking, I know the feeling, especially at auditions when I feel there's not a prayer of getting the job. Looking up, she says the line. Then she looks down for her next line—"I'm unhappy"—and thinks, This is me today because I hate what I'm doing. Or maybe she's not unhappy. That is also usable, as long as she says the line of the script. After all, Masha may be reluctant to say this. She may be irritated by the question. Who knows? The important thing is to see where the line and her feelings at the moment take Sophie. They are all that she has.

I listen to what she says. I think it's kind of theatrical, using words like "mourning," "wearing black." Then, breathing in and out, I look down at my line, "Why?" I'm curious. I've forgotten where I'm going even though I know this play very well. So I look down at my next line. "I don't understand . . ." Making sure I don't rush, I take a breath and look for the rest of the line, "You are in good health." I breathe out, look up, and say the line. It feels foolish to me. I look down, breathe in and out—letting the next line into myself—look up and say, "And your father, though not rich, is well off." I know this may seem absurd, but I feel like one of my uncles when I say this—like an old man. The next line is "My life is much harder than yours." Breathing, feeling like a complete fool, I look up and say it. I'm embarrassed by my line. But I say what I feel. I have no idea how it's coming out of my mouth. I only know what's playing on me. I don't care if it makes sense. This is just an exploration. There will be many more. I'm only concerned with this moment.

"I get only twenty-three rubles a month." I find myself getting angry with the self-pity in the line. "And out of that they take something for the pension fund." I want to shout this, I feel so stupid and angry. I look up and let it out, almost shouting. I look down. "But I don't wear mourning." I spit this out!

The actress is shocked. Looking down, she reads, "It's not a question of money." Breathing out, she says this to me as if I'm an idiot. "Even a beggar can be happy," she says dismissively.

As she is talking, I'm thinking, Beggar?! I get my line: "Yes, in theory." She is ridiculous, not me, I think. "But in practice it's like this." I get the line out quickly, brutally. "There's my mother, my two sisters, and a little brother." My eye picks this up all at once, because my mind is moving very fast. It's hard to slow down. "On a salary of only twenty-three rubles." It comes popping out of me, full of frustration and anger. "People have to eat and drink, don't they?" Getting louder. "And they need tea and sugar? And tobacco?" Finally I let the anger leave me. I make sure to breathe in and out so I can take my time and let the next line in simply. "It's not easy to make ends meet." I feel humiliated, apologetic.

And so on.

It may seem to beginning actors that I and other experienced actors must have unrestricted access to our feelings and fantasies. But sometimes even seasoned performers have difficulty exploring the lines freely because their physical self-consciousness is keeping them from feeling connected to what they are saying.

Actors are physical creatures, and it is necessary for them to feel physically free in order for their instinct and imagination to surface on a given line. Yet most physical training in acting has to do with the nonverbal—mime, clown technique, dance. A great deal of actor training in avant-garde theater, games theater, and methods of study like that of the French teacher LeCoq emphasizes physical improvisation. All of this is valuable. But for most actors, the simple relationship between physical ease and ease in speaking lines is more immediately important. If the actor feels a separation between his physical and verbal expression, he will be blocked emotionally as well as creatively. All he will feel is self-conscious and awkward about moving and talking on stage or before the camera. The lack of connection will make everything he says or every move he makes feel unnatural to him.

Film actors in particular tend to suffer from this disconnect. As Ally Sheedy told me, "I had this fear of using my body. Most of the time you don't use it in film. Nobody said to move your body. They usually said, 'Stand on your mark' or 'Just walk from there to there and say the line.' I would disconnect from my body and just use my head."

You may recall that in Paul's monologue from *Loose Ends*, when I read the line "Teach us songs," I had an impulse to physicalize the image: I danced and sang, and felt that I could touch the words and image. As I physicalized the image, it became easier to say the phrase, because I already felt connected to it, and my body felt comfortable. In fact, I was not aware of any tension in my body because I was consumed by the image itself. I did this not with the intention of physicalizing the image or line in performance, but in order to explore the text and character without being self-conscious. I often have to physicalize an image for myself before I can freely say it while taking the lines off the page. I'm very tactile and need to *touch* the image to make it real for me.

I ask an actor who is having difficulty taking it off the page because he is physically self-conscious to do the same thing. First he looks down and lets the line into himself while breathing in and out. Then I have him physicalize the image for himself in such a way that he feels he can almost touch it. Then, after he has physicalized the image, he says the line. As with the actor's reactions when speaking, it doesn't matter how foolish or stupid the physicalizing is. It's not for performance. And after the actor has done it once, he may not need to do it again. As a matter of fact, in performance the actor may not move at all. This physicalizing is for the actor, so that he can feel the image in his body and then say the line or phrase with the writer's words. Once he's gotten it out of his body, he is free to repeat it or not, whatever interests him.

Ally remembers it this way: "Before I said a word, I had to physicalize it through my body. I had to say it physically before I could verbalize the word, the image." She adds, "It was the hardest thing for me to do at that point. It was just so foreign to use my body while acting. I was at loose ends. I had been a dancer, and it was like stretching this muscle I hadn't used for so long. But it all came back."

Remember earlier in the chapter when I described to Ellen my response to her line, "He died from champagne"? I mimed for myself sniffing the bubbles in a champagne glass that I imagined holding. This kind of physicalization can help us to respond and feel what we say.

Once the actor connects the physical to the specific image and thought in a way that is freeing, his imagination and instinct will take over. His body will again feel natural to him. He will be fully expressive. It is not necessary to do this with every phrase or line, only those that cause him trouble.

If the actor is having particular difficulty freeing himself physically while he is taking it off the page, I may ask him to move after each phrase—walk to another chair or across the room, lean against the wall or sit on the floor or lie down. Once he comes to rest, he can breathe in and out, let the next line in, physicalize the image (or not), and then say the phrase. After he says it, I ask him to change his position again before he goes to the next line, and so on. The choice of where and how to move each time is arbitrary— the actor must move without thinking. Then he must settle into a *quiet place* before he picks up the next line. In this way, the stillness becomes physical as well.

Even Kevin Kline, who is now considered a physical acting genius, had to learn to trust his immediate physical responses, because at first they seemed so outrageous. He thought he would seem foolish if he acted on them. But he gave a memorable demonstration of how physical and verbal impulses interact when he was preparing his first Hamlet at the Public Theater in New York. Sitting on my couch, Kevin was taking "To be or not to be" off the page. He looked down at the page for a long time, took a breath in and out, looked up, and said quietly, "To be," as if he was trying to figure out what he was saying. Instead of continuing with the rest of the line, which of course he knew, he looked at the line as if he had never seen it before. He took a breath in and out and looked up. He didn't say anything. He got up, walked toward me, and pointed to a foot-long conductor's baton sitting on the bookshelf over my desk.

"May I?" he asked.

"Sure," I said.

He took the baton and sat on the edge of the sofa. Then, with his index finger, he touched the vulnerable flesh on the right side of his neck just under the jawbone. He placed the point of the baton there and balanced the other end precariously on the middle finger of his right hand, pushing the baton's sharp point gently into the soft skin of his neck. His head tilted back, his neck totally exposed to the point, he breathed in and out and said, "or not to be." The phrase came out so simply, yet with full consciousness of how easy it would be to push the point through his neck if it were a razor-sharp dagger rather than a plastic baton.

He continued taking phrase after phrase off the page with the baton against his throat. It was thrilling and terrifying for me and for him.

Kevin needed something to spark or free his imagination so he could say the lines of this famous soliloquy and take responsibility for them. While taking it off the page, he had given himself the time to let his mind, his instincts—and his eyes—wander. He felt instinctively that he needed a physical component to these thoughts. That's why and how he spotted the conductor's baton. In being available to his thoughts, his feelings, his imagination, and his physicality, an actor also becomes available to serendipitous discovery.

As Prince Hal says in Shakespeare's *Henry IV, Part I*, "And nothing pleaseth but rare accidents."

Suggestions for Practice

Practice taking it off the page with a monologue, *not* a scene, at first. If you get used to trusting yourself and your responses to your own lines, you will find that scenes are much easier. That is because in a scene the stimulus for the response comes from outside—from the other actor. So you are pushed to respond. But immersing yourself in a monologue, relying only on yourself and the text, will make you much stronger and independent in scenes with other actors. You won't be at the mercy of the other actor. Although you have no choice over what you hear, see, feel, and think when the other actor is saying his line, you are free after responding to drop that response and go wherever your own line takes you. So, the stronger you are and the more available to yourself, the better for your development in the long run.

I suggest young men start with Tuzenbach's Act I monologue in Chekhov's *The Three Sisters*. It begins: "The longing for work, oh, my God, how well I understand it!"

I suggest young women start with Irina's Act I monologue in *The Three Sisters*. It begins: "Tell me, why am I so happy today?" Cut Ivan Romanych's line "My little white bird . . ." and end with the line: "And if I don't get up early and work, you can give me up as a friend, Ivan Romanych."

Both these monologues will be helpful in beginning your work because they are full of interesting language and images for physicalization, and very emotional. Both monologues can also be naïve, foolish, idiotic, and fun as well as passionate. If you trust yourself to let the phrases, lines, and images into yourself without acting you will find yourself, step-by-step, slipping into the character's shoes. Don't try to speak better than you do. Use your own voice—this will keep you in touch with yourself as you explore the text.

Work on your first monologue every day for at least a week or until the lines come to you without looking down at the page. Don't try to memorize. Don't try to run the lines. Just take it off the page from beginning to end until you feel used up, frustrated, or unable to concentrate. Then stop working on the monologue for the moment. Don't force it. Do something else for a while— take a walk, have a cup of tea or a snack. Do something that will refresh you, not tire you out. Then, when you're clear, go back to the monologue. Do this several times a day, even if you can only work for twenty minutes or half an hour without a break. You will find that each time you work you will have real concentration, even if it's just for a short time. And going back again and again will extend your concentration, until you can work for longer and longer periods. Training your concentration is one of the most important things you can do as an actor.

After the first day, read the whole play. It's a long play and you may not be used to reading this kind of writing, so go slowly. Never read for speed; it may be valuable in academic work, but it is useless for actors. While reading, keep going back to the monologue, taking the lines off the page several times each day.

Obsess over your work—it's good for you. For instance, Ellen Wolf told me that she leaves her script on the kitchen table. She often works in there, cooking, cleaning, opening the mail, and a lot of varied emotions pop up there—she cuts her finger, reads an annoying letter, receives a rotten or wonderful phone call, creates a fantastic dinner (or blows it). Whatever is happening, she picks up the script and starts on the monologue or the scene. In this way, she starts not from a set place, ready to Act, but from within her life, her everyday experiences. She allows them to inform the text. This is a very good way to work.

Remember, don't make taking it off the page a Technique. Stay loose! Most important, take the time to breathe in and out before you say the line. Then say it before thinking about it. The breathing will give you plenty of time to register the thought or image. Let the line take you as it comes out of your mouth. At first, take the line off the page in pieces. When in doubt, stop and take a breath in and out. Then go on to the next piece.

Don't make decisions. Don't hold on to something just because it worked once. Keep exploring each time you go back to the monologue. Keep letting go—and keep going. Trust that things that are good will come back and things that don't work will fall away.

It's more important to know what feels free than to know what is right. The sense of being arbitrary is what we are after—*not caring* what works or where we are going but rather feeling free to test our wings and do whatever comes to us from the line.

If you are feeling "stuck" or if you are thinking too much before saying the line, first try physicalizing the line while taking it off the page. Then, try *moving arbitrarily* to another place in the room before saying the line. Without reading, move (to another chair, down on the floor, against the wall), come to rest, then look down at the phrase—*not* the whole line—while breathing, physicalize (or not) and say it. Keep doing this until you are no longer stuck or thinking too much.

If you are boring yourself with your work on the monologue, try this: do the whole monologue from beginning to end five different ways—first do it for laughs, then for interior values, then for anger, then for tenderness, and then for petty (bratty) values. Finally, after exploring the monologue in each of these ways, do it however it comes out. You may surprise yourself with entirely new responses.

After spending a week or more on your first monologue, move on to a second one. Men should work on Chekhov's *The Seagull*, Treplev's monologue in Act I, starting with the line "She loves me—she loves me not," and going all the way to "I could guess their thoughts and I suffered from humiliation." (Cut Sorin's line, "We can't do without the theater.")

Women should work on Elena's soliloquy in Chekhov's *Uncle Vanya*, Act III, starting with the line, "There is nothing worse than knowing someone's secret and not being able to help."

These monologues are more difficult and more complicated, but work on them the same way, taking the lines off the page in pieces, allowing yourself to breathe and say what you mean and feel without caring where you are going or whether you are right or wrong. Let each moment take you rather than you taking it.

After working a day or two on your monologue, start to read the entire play, slowly. Keep working on the monologue several times a day for a week or two until the lines are coming to you without reading. Do not memorize!

You may notice that I begin with plays by Chekhov that many think too difficult for young actors. I disagree. I believe this material is excellent for young actors because Chekhov's characters go all over the place. They are full of emotion and passion. They can be trivial, silly, and foolish one moment and poetic or profound the next. And his characters are always verbal. This is a good introduction to the real art of acting, I believe. I find that actors work better and faster with truly thought-provoking material—it gives them a stimulating environment. The actor will absorb whatever he can take in. No matter how little it may be, it will still be more useful to his development than working on lesser material. And once the actor is free with complex material, everything else is easy.

After a week or two, go on to a third monologue: for the men, in Sam Shepard's *The Tooth of Crime*, Hoss's monologue in Act I, starting with the line, "Once I knew this cat in High School who was a Creole"; for the women, in John Guare's play *Marco Polo Sings a Solo*, Diane's monologue beginning with the line, "I really started cookin' when I was eight."

These are very different kinds of characters and monologues. They are quite fun and complicated, and rich in images to stimulate the actor's imagination. You will find them invaluable for opening yourself to physicalizing, exploring the outrageous, and connecting you to your instinct, imagination, and emotions. After a day or so, read the play.

While working in depth on the monologues I have suggested, add a new monologue each day for practice. Repeat the new monologue twice. The next day, go on to another monologue. Add a new monologue each day for six weeks, but continue working in depth on the original monologues, reading the plays, and allowing yourself to grow with the character.

You will find that the process gets easier and faster each day, leaving you feeling more natural and free each time you begin your work on a new text or prepare for an audition.

Following is a list of monologues that have been valuable for many of the young actors I have taught. The order I have put them in suggests a rough path, but feel free to vary the order or add different monologues that interest you.

MEN	WOMEN
Chekhov, *The Three Sisters*	Chekhov, *The Three Sisters*
Tuzenbach in Act I	Irina in Act I
"The longing for work . . ."	"Tell me, why am I so happy?"
Chekhov, *The Seagull*	Chekhov, *Uncle Vanya*
Treplev in Act I	Elena in Act III
"She loves me . . ."	"There's nothing worse . . ."
Sam Shepard, *The Tooth of Crime*	John Guare, *Marco Polo Sings a Solo*
Hoss in Act I	"I really started cooking when I was
"Once I knew this cat in High School . . ."	eight . . ."
Michael Weller, *Loose Ends*	Sam Shepard, *Cowboy Mouth*
Paul in scene I	Cavale
"It was great at the beginning . . ."	"I know the rhythm of it . . ."
Chekhov, *The Seagull*	Chekhov, *The Three Sisters*
Treplev in Act II	Irina in Act II
"This began the evening my play failed . . ."	"Here I am, home at last . . ." Cut Masha and Tuzenbach's lines.

Arthur Miller, *Death of a Salesman*
Happy in Act I
From "That's what I long for . . . " to
" . . . I take it and—I love it. "

Shakespeare, *King Lear*
Edgar in Act II, scene 3
"I heard myself proclaimed . . . "

Eugene O'Neil, *Long Day's Journey into Night*
Edmund in Act IV
"Don't lie about it!"

Shakespeare, *Romeo and Juliet*
Romeo in Act II, scene 2
"He jests at scars . . . "

Michael Weller, *Loose Ends*
Janice in scene 7
"Like with Russel . . . "

Shakespeare, *As You Like It*
Phebe in Act III, scene 5
"Think not I love him . . . "

Chekhov, *Uncle Vanya*
Sonya in Act II "He didn't say" anything . . . "
Attach Act III, "When a woman is not
beautiful . . . "

Shakespeare, *Romeo and Juliet*
Juliet in Act II, scene 2
"Thou knowest the mask of night . . . "

Other Recommended Monologues

MEN

Arthur Miller, *Death of a Salesman*
Biff in Act I
"I spent six or seven years . . . " to
" . . . all I've done is to waste my
life . . . " Cut Hap's line.

Sam Shepard, *Buried Child*
Vince in Act III
"I was gonna run last night . . . "

WOMEN

Michael Weller, *Loose Ends*
Susan in scene 1
"You got another cigarette?" and "OK,
when I was ten . . . "

Sam Shepard, *Cowboy Mouth*
Cavale
"You're so neat."

Eugene O'Neill, *Long Days Journey into Night*
Edmund in Act I, scene 2
"Yes, she moves above and beyond us . . ."

Chekhov, *The Seagull*
Masha in Act III
"I'm telling you all this because you're a writer . . . " Cut Trigorin's lines and make a monologue out of her lines in the scene.

Chekhov, *The Three Sisters*
Irina in Act III
"Yes, how shallow our Andrei has become" to "I'm not crying anymore. Enough. " Cut all other's lines.

Shakespeare, *Twelfth Night*
Olivia in Act I, scene 5
"What is your parentage?" to end of Act I. Cut Malvolio's lines.

After a few weeks, you may want to start working on a scene with a partner. You will also find in chapter 3 a way to prepare scenes on your own.

When working with a partner, do your own work—taking the lines off the page and looking up while listening to the other actor. It is best not to impose your way of working on the other actor. Simply do your work, and let the other actor do his. Don't talk too much about the scene and how it should go. It's not necessary to discuss it if you have felt it. Just keep reading the scene back and forth, exploring freely. Let the scene take you to lots of places. Get up from the table when you feel ready. Be free with your movement—be arbitrary. Don't memorize. If you let the lines come to you, it will happen on its own.

Following is a list of scenes that you might find useful in starting your work with a partner.

Man / Woman	Arthur Miller, *A View From the Bridge*
	Catherine and Rodolpho in Act II
Man / Man	Arthur Miller, *Death of a Salesman*
	Biff and Happy in Act I
Woman / Woman	Anton Chekhov, *Uncle Vanya*
	Elena and Sonya in Act II
	Start "The storm is over . . . "
Man / Woman	Anton Chekhov, *The Seagull*
	Medvedenko and Masha in Act I
	Opening scene
Man / Woman	Michael Weller, *Loose Ends*
	Paul and Susan in scene 5
	Start "Want some more?"
Woman / Woman	Shakespeare, *Twelfth Night*
	Viola and Olivia in Act I, scene 5
Man / Woman	Shakespeare, *Measure for Measure*
	Isabella and Angelo in Act II, scene 4

2

EXPLORING THE ROLE TO UNCOVER THE CHARACTER

"Acting is finding the truth. Some truths are more important than other truths. Some truths resonate and some are just intellectual notions. Good acting is when it is a truth that is intellectually and absolutely inspired—something personal and transcendent that moves you. That's what we are talking about. It is the truth that is important to you—the truth that is personal in a profound way."

—Kevin Kline

Some actors like to start from the outside of the character. What does the character look like—is he thin or fat, light or dark, physically fit or unfit? How does the character dress—formal or informal, neat or sloppy? Is the character rich, middle-class, poor? Is he educated? How does he speak? Walk? Eat? This is important stuff to know, and I deal with all these aspects of character eventually when I'm coaching an actor. But I don't start there.

American actors are usually taught to start with the inside of the character, as Stanislavski did. The "art" that teaches us to "create consciously and rightly" is supposed to begin with the conscious analysis of the character's motivations. Analysis of the script entails defining the character's objective—what the character wants—in each scene. This motivates the character's action. There may also be several smaller objectives within the scene that the actor must define in active terms to take him toward his larger objective. Stanislavski stressed above all the need to know the character's super-objective—the character's "larger, vital purpose" in life or throughout the play. He believed that "the whole stream of individual minor objectives, all the imaginative thoughts, feelings, and actions of an actor, should converge to carry out the super-objective of the plot." This analysis of the play for the character's objectives and super-objective is the actor's "conscious" work.

As I have pointed out, however, all this analytical work interferes with the actor's access to his unconscious instinct and feeling. He knows too much about the character in advance, and his thinking interferes with inspiration. Even Stanislavski observes, "When the subconscious, when intuition, enters into our work we must know how not to interfere." But rather than abandon the analytic approach, he developed a "special technique" to re-create in the actor the emotions he had worked out for his character.

The "special technique," known as emotional recall or sense memory, goes something like this: the actor searches his memory for experiences in his past that evoked responses in him that are akin to the responses he has settled upon for his character. Then he goes through the experiences, detail by detail, to rekindle the attendant reactions, feelings, and senses. He plugs these into his performance at the appropriate moments in the text and practices accessing the responses so that they will appear in performance when they are needed.

The idea is to be able to evoke these responses consistently, at the same points in every performance. Stanislavski quotes the great actor of his time, Salvini, as saying, "The great actor . . . must feel an emotion not only once or twice while he is studying his part, but to a greater or lesser degree every time he plays it, no matter whether it is the first or the thousandth time." Then Stanislavski writes, "Unfortunately this is not within our control. Our subconscious is inaccessible to our consciousness. We cannot enter into that realm. If for any reason we do penetrate into it, then the subconscious becomes conscious and dies." He believed, however, that he could "rouse the subconscious to creative work" through his "special technique," training the actor to produce consistent, authentic responses.

This is what is generally defined as the Method, and today there are many expert teachers of it, each with variations of his own. Most American actors started out acting in this way, including me. But I have long since abandoned starting there in my own acting or when I coach other actors, despite my great love for Stanislavski's work. I appreciate how radical and forward-thinking he was for his time. He formulated his ideas about acting in the late nineteenth century, when Chekhov, Dostoyevski, and Strindberg were writing and Freud was on the verge of making his theories known. He developed his "special technique" in reaction to the general acting style of his day, which was all elegant movement, elocution, and overly dramatic displays of characters' emotions that bore not a touch of truthfulness.

But we are not the children of Stanislavski's theatre, and as contemporary actors and audiences, we take it for granted that acting should be real and natural. The best acting in theater should be no different from the best acting in film. And to my mind, the best is no acting at all, just real characters full of the variety and complexity of life.

Stanislavski says, "One cannot always create subconsciously and with inspiration. No such genius exists in the world. Therefore our art teaches us first of all to create consciously and rightly, because that will best prepare the way for the blossoming of the subconscious, which is inspiration. The more you have of conscious creative moments in your role, the more chance you will have of a flow of inspiration."

As I acted in production after production, I came to believe that this was not true for me. Rather than freeing my inspiration, the conscious intellectual choices I made about my characters obligated me, closing down my instinct as well as my feelings. I worked hard at Stanislavski's technique to find the emotions I needed to fill the character, but it didn't truly work for me. It pulled me away from my true, free response to the script and the moment. By forcing me to favor memory over imagination, it shut down my connection to my unconscious thoughts, images, and fantasies. Using the technique always left me outside the intimate connection to the moment on stage or film. It took me out of the scene. I could always feel the gears turning. I felt as if I was in my own separate world, apart from the play going on around me. And the emotion never felt free. I was Acting.

But when I rejected analysis and technique, I found that my imagination was free, full, and available to me again, and surprisingly, so were my emotions—without prolonged work on emotional recall. They were inspired by my moment by moment improvisation on the line, using nothing but my intuition and the script. And best of all, my connection to the words I spoke was natural, easy, and stimulating.

I have no quarrel with actors who use the Method—or any other technique—if it works for them. I never try to change them. Every actor must find what works for him. I deal with the problems actors present to me, not what is working well. But many actors have come to me with a sense of being cut off from their instinct and imagination, just as I was. Or they come with a vague sense that something isn't working, believing that the inadequacy lies with them, not the technique. And over the years I have watched many actors struggling to push their emotions, not trusting the text in the moment.

I also believe that many actors who work well don't really work in the prescribed way. They may not tell you that. They may not even know how they work—which can be a very good thing, because they are not bogged down with an Approach. But they don't work in the prescribed way, because they need a freer access to instinct and themselves. They need to trust themselves more than their technique.

To the extent that I believe in an Approach, I think that for many—perhaps most—actors the process works in a way opposite to the Method: if the actor accesses the subconscious *first*, through his uncensored response to the character's words, he is inspired to explore the character in a creative and surprising way. I have found that it is next to impossible for the actor to "first create consciously." In fact, the more conscious moments the actor has, I believe, the *less* chance he has of experiencing a flow of inspiration. Any time our thinking is too neat, it flattens our instinct. We have no true feelings because we have to fit our feelings into the way we see the character.

So how do I think about character?

In *An Actor Prepares*, Stanislavski writes, "Acting with your subconscious, intuitively . . . [is] very good, *if* your intuition carries you along the right path, and very bad if it makes a mistake."

The caveat makes us panic at the possibility of making a mistake. It stresses the *right path*. But what is the right path? Is it the decision we make while analyzing the script? This is an intellectual decision based on a technique more appropriate to the classroom. This has nothing to do with art. The writer, if good, is writing from an instinctive, creative place. We, as actors, have to deal with his writing in an instinctive and creative way. And who is to decide what is the right path?

I have come to believe that the "consistency" Stanislavski valued so highly is not necessary, or even desirable. It is certainly not worth the loss of spontaneity, if that is what it costs the actor.

And I don't see the conception of character as a finite thing. The character is not some painted-on picture of what we have decided in rehearsal, then presented as a finished product to the audience. The character is simply the actor's continual responses to the author's lines, an ongoing exploration that remains completely personal for him, from first reading through final performance.

The character has to be in us if the audience is ever to believe us, and if we want to be free and alive in each moment. After all, the lines are coming out of our mouths anyway. *We want the audience to be lost in what we say and do*, not standing back, judging whether we are acting the character well or badly. So the lines must be ours, or the audience will see us acting a character. And every moment must be us—really us, what we are personally thinking, seeing, feeling, and saying. That is why the audience believes it and feels it. That's what I mean when I say we must take responsibility for the line.

But the actor doesn't have to take responsibility for the character in the same way. The way the action and lines go from one line to the next, and one action to the next, creates the character. The actor's responses remain in pieces, changing moment by moment, and with each repetition. *They come together as the character only for the audience*, as the lines, action, and story unfold before them in performance. *That is not the actor. The moments are the actor. The character is the text.* Because the script, the action, and the story are complete—finite—the actor does not have to be. In fact, I believe he *must not be*, in order for the character and script to be alive. The actor must be continually exploring the role by freely responding to the dialogue before rehearsal, in rehearsal, and—I know this a controversial notion—*throughout his performance on stage or in filming.*

That is why I make such a big deal of starting one's work with the line—taking the line off the page and into oneself. As you will start to see, this idea of character is an extension of taking it off the page. We not only start there, we end there.

There is no difference for me between *exploring* the role and *playing* the character. Everything I do in my coaching is about freeing the actor to explore the character, continually and spontaneously. That, to me, is what acting is all about.

In later chapters, I will explore the specific problems actors encounter in theater, in film, and in television—problems that block the actor's ability to freely explore the character. This chapter presents a strategy to maximize the actor's instinct, imagination, and emotions in order to become the character in any of these arenas.

As actors, we are always searching for the truth—the truth of the character, of the script, and of ourselves. But as Kevin Kline so gracefully puts it, "Some truths are more important than other truths." The truth that we are searching for is the one that will leave us free to explore creatively throughout the process, from first reading through performance. That is why not all truths are valuable for the actor—only the ones that stimulate him personally.

When I have let the lines of the character into me, I feel I am inside the character as well as myself. And once I have done that, I find that these characters often talk to me while I'm taking their thoughts and images off the page. Sometimes they tell me I'm wearing the wrong clothes when I'm saying their lines. "Why are you wearing sneakers when I'm talking?" they'll say, or, "Why are you talking so loud and fast?"

I know it's my imagination playing tricks on me. But I listen. I never question it, because I also know it's my instinct at work and I'm just exploring. I *let* the character talk to me, tell me what to do, not only when I'm taking it off the page but as I'm walking down the street or talking about the character to a friend. In fact, I want this to happen. That's why I start my work by verbalizing the character's lines. So my instinct and imagination are in connection to his words, so he will talk to me. It sounds simplistic but I trust that.

At the same time, the actor can't force this. Choices like rhythms and character traits must be explored continually by trying out different choices while preparing and performing. The good choices keep coming back even when the actor is not trying to repeat them, and the bad choices are so obvious to the actor that he's the first to know it. He can hear it as it comes out of his mouth, or feel it when he makes a false move.

It takes a lot of courage not to settle things early. Actors always feel pressured to come up with results. But rushing only makes their choices predictable.

By opening yourself up to the character by taking his lines off the page, you give the character a chance to affect you early in the process. That's what the actor needs to start his work of finding himself in the character. Everything that happens in our work must be coming directly from the character's words and actions. But sometimes the character isn't talking to us.

For instance, Bridget Fonda found herself "having a hard time" as she was preparing her character, Maggie, in *Point of No Return*. We had been reading the script back and forth, and it was not working for her. She couldn't find the anger behind Maggie's actions—killing a policeman who was trying to help her, as well as creating bloody havoc wherever she went. Maggie is young, violent, uncivilized. Her lines didn't feel true in Bridget's mouth, and her behavior felt unreal to Bridget.

So we stopped to talk about this young woman.

"I remember discovering the essence of the character while working with you one day," Bridget told me. "The question was how do you maintain a sense of compassion for so vicious a character? It was very hard for me. How do I have so much rage and horrific behavior and do it honestly and yet still feel for this person?

"Basically, I thought of this character as an attack dog who has been discarded. She had been trained to be distrustful, vicious—a puppy born into a world where someone mistreats it over and over and over again so it doesn't trust anybody. It becomes a guard dog—unhappy, bereft, and unable to trust anything good. It's ruined. And yet, the dog wants to belong. It can't. It was this perfectly neurotic state of being that I needed. And it completely informed everything. It was the only way I could be all those things."

Maggie had not been talking to Bridget because she couldn't find "a sense of compassion for this character" until that day. Once she found that—an emotional truth that really spoke to her—she was in tune with the character and free to follow her instinct. "I became less scared—to the point where I was bossy on set. 'I've got to do it like this—let me show you!' Which is what you want at that point."

Once the character is really talking to you, you're on your way. Gradually, in the response moment by moment, the character becomes clear to you. There's a sense of the character in your body, in your reactions, in your words. But you must not force it. If we trust what we hear from the character and from ourselves, the script will take us the rest of the way. We will feel it and not have to act it.

Actors always want to know how I come up with interesting and creative takes on characters, characters that aren't like me as I appear in daily life and that aren't like each other. It's simple: I let the lines and images connect with my imagination. I don't worry about consistency; I let myself respond moment by moment, piecemeal, to the character's dialogue and actions. Then I let my responses take me wherever they go, making mistakes and discarding them until choices start repeating themselves on their own no matter how arbitrary they seem at first. Then I know I'm on to something. But I don't try to put the character together. I leave it in pieces. The script and story put the character together so my moment by moment performance seems like a creative take on the whole character.

Of course, something usually gets in the way of this process. I can see where the character is going when I read the script. Or I think I know what will be expected of me. Or I fall into a comfortable, familiar pattern of speaking or moving. Or I feel that I already know the character too well—which, believe it or not, can be a serious handicap.

Work from the Negative

The most effective way I know of getting through these obstacles is to *work from the negative.* In order to find out what a character is, I have first got to find out what he is not, exploring without fear or self-censorship. Exploring the role is like sculpting in marble. There is a huge block of marble. The character is somewhere inside this block. All the actor has to do is get rid of the marble that doesn't belong. What he is left with is the character, and it's himself. Then the actor is the character. And he doesn't have to act!

If I find a right choice for the character in my exploration, it still may not be the best choice. But if I find a wrong choice, one that doesn't work, then I know something about the character. The character is not that! When I find a truth I can't negate, then I'm home free with this character—I can stop thinking and just play him. I don't have to Act. But how do I know a wrong choice is wrong? I know when the choice doesn't do anything for me. I get it out and it just plain feels wrong. That's part of my instinct as an actor. A director may disagree, but it makes no difference. If it feels wrong, it's wrong. Nothing will make it right. If I continue to do it, I will have to fake it, Act it.

A right choice is right because it does something for me. I feel it in my bones. But I may not be finished. There may be a better choice ahead for me. So I keep exploring.

How do I know when a choice is the best and have it play on me throughout the many scenes I have to act? I think of it this way: something that seems right about the character may pop up in my work. I don't say this is what the character is yet, because I'm just exploring. But if it keeps popping up, at a certain point, my focus becomes clear. I sense who the character is underneath!

I know and feel who this character *is*, but not *how* I am going to act it. Eventually, though, the character is inside me. So it doesn't matter what scene I am doing at the moment, the *thing* that kept popping up in my exploration is playing unconsciously in the scene as well.

Bridget told me that in *Single White Female* she didn't want to play a victim. "I wanted to play this person who was completely unconscious of how she was bringing everything down onto herself," she told me. "It was beneath the lines, but there was room for it.

"If there's something that's hidden, in the moment of trying to make a scene work on the surface, I can forget my deeper [hidden] course of action. Through constant exposure, it's become ingrained and planted a seed in my core. That won't be washed away by a 'surface-y' little scene."

Often, the best way of starting to work from the negative is to do the opposite of what conventional wisdom suggests. If I see what the character should be, or if I know how most actors would play him, or if I'm playing a role made famous by an actor— Brando's Stanley in *A Streetcar Named Desire*, or Olivier's Henry V—I invariably head straight off in the opposite direction. By negating what I see and know, I put myself in a no-man's land where almost anything is possible, because I only know what I'm *not* going to do.

Let's return to the character of Masha in Chekhov's *The Seagull* as an example.

As we saw in the last chapter, Masha's first line is, "I'm in mourning for my life. I'm unhappy." In Act II she is described by the writer Trigorin: "Takes snuff and drinks vodka . . . always in black." She is the daughter of an overbearing, unaffectionate man who is the steward of the estate. Masha's mother is not in love with him, and is somewhat openly in love with the doctor, Dorn, who does not return her affections. Masha grew up on the estate with Konstantin Treplev, the son of the great actress Arkadina and nephew of Sorin, who owns the estate. She is in love with him. But Konstantin not only doesn't love her, he barely notices her existence. Masha's love is as unrequited as her mother's.

So it is easy to see Masha as a depressed person who hates her life and is always unhappy. And this is how most actors play the character—dark and teary. They may even do research on depression and the effects it has on personality, and then try to play Masha in what they think is the *right way*, stuffing the facts they have discovered into the performance.

Unquestionably, depression is a truth about the character. But is it a truth that can sustain the actor's interest in exploring and playing the role? I think research has its place, which I'll discuss later. But to approach the behavior of any character as a case study seems too single-minded, too obvious, too binding, and not stimulating enough for me. So I negate that choice. Then I am free to go deep into my imagination, thoughts, and feelings. Once I am working on instinct, I can use anything that strikes me for Masha, ultimately even those things I negated at first—things I discover from research or from other actors' portrayals, or things I rejected as being too obvious.

So how might one explore Masha? Work from the negative. Suppose that, instead of hating her "dark and dreary" life, she embraces it. She is used to misfortune, she grew up with it and she's comfortable with it. Could she see her unrequited love as making her special—a romance novel heroine in her own eyes? After all, unlike her mother and many other women, she drinks and uses snuff openly, to boldly distinguish herself. Maybe she sees herself as an individualist and she's proud of it—a woman breaking the rules for women. She has a tragic purpose. Here's how it might play out in the moment:

At the beginning of Act III, Masha jokes to Trigorin, "I'm telling you all this because you're a writer. You may be able to use it." She could become the tragic heroine of his next novel. Yes, she's unhappy about her lovelessness, but she can be dramatic about it, or at least self-dramatizing. Her drinking allows her to weep openly, to laugh, to rage one moment and be sexy and flirtatious the next. Instead of whining about her life as her mother does, she jokes wryly at her own expense. I find her a fascinating character who can be unpredictable—childlike, cynical, thoughtful, petulant, realistic, and yet lost in her fantasies.

Masha continues her conversation with Trigorin, referring to

Konstantin's recent attempt at suicide. She says, "I tell you honestly: if he had seriously wounded himself, I would not have gone on living another minute." In *my* imagination, she heard the gunshot and ran to Konstantin, fearing he had finally killed himself over the loss of Nina's love and intending to shoot herself with the same gun so she could die next to him, proving her love for him even into eternity. The beauty and tragedy of the image are still enough to make her weep. But Konstantin had only grazed his head with the bullet, and his failure at suicide left her to face her own stupidity and inner rage.

"But I have courage all the same," she says angrily. "I've made up my mind to tear this love out of my heart—" she tries to stop her tears "—tear it out by the roots."

Trigorin asks, "How are you going to do that?"

She takes another drink, hums "Here Comes the Bride," and answers lightly, "I'm going to get married. To Medvedenko." She knows this choice is foolish, so she jokes about it. But then she says, about this doomed unloving choice she has to make, "To love without hope . . . " and, going deeply into her pain, "to spend whole years waiting for something . . . " and then, trying to convince herself it makes sense, "But when I marry, there'll be no more of that, new cares will stifle the old." She's too smart to believe this, however. She becomes bored with her own tears and tosses off, "Anyhow, it will be a change. Shall we have another?"

Oh, God, how she needs a drink. As she pours, she notices his disapproval and laughs it off. "Oh, come! Women drink more often than you can imagine. Only a few drink openly as I do, the rest do it in secret and it's always vodka or cognac. Good luck." And down the hatch it goes.

There is a truth to both ways of looking at Masha. And of course there are possibilities beyond either. But if we are too quick to jump to analysis, we are apt to go with the obvious assessment, and the character may from the outset be too familiar for us to explore with any feeling, interest, or freedom. If we negate that choice, we may discover a second possibility, or a number of others. Unsure of where we are going, we allow instinct and our imagination to take us to places we didn't expect. The mystery of the character creates possibilities that will be a joy to explore.

Use the Double Negative

Working from the negative means negating not only what you assume a character *is* but also what you assume he is *not*. For example, if you are playing Stanley Kowalski in Tennessee Williams's *A Streetcar Named Desire*, you may take it as a given that Stanley is an insensitive lout. But the only way to find out if he is not sensitive is to try out the possibility that he is.

Let's take the scene where Stanley possibly overhears Blanche describing him as an animal to his wife, Stella. Blanche says, "Don't hang back with the brutes." Is it possible that Stanley pretends he hasn't overheard, in order to hide how devastated he is at being described this way, even by someone he doesn't like? This could open up some interesting qualities that aren't immediately apparent. Stanley could turn out to be a "brute" with delicate feelings—a vulnerable brute. If the actor tests it, he will find out. If it doesn't work, the actor will know it in his gut, not just his head, and he will throw it away. But if he thinks a choice is wrong and doesn't try it out, it will continue to play on him until he does. Always explore a wrong choice that strikes you in some way—that comes into your head and keeps intruding on your impulses. It is like a repressed feeling that wreaks havoc until it is uncovered and dealt with. You might as well get it out as soon as it comes to you. And if by chance this "wrong" choice works, it will probably be not just a good but a great choice, because it is so unexpected.

Make Strong Choices

Aidan Quinn told me about an early rehearsal of *A Streetcar Named Desire* when he was playing Stanley at the Circle in the Square revival. At the very beginning of the play, Stanley comes on stage bellowing, "Hey there! Stella, baby!"

"Don't holler at me like that," Stella says.

"Catch!" Stanley yells.

"What?"

"Meat!"

As he yelled "Catch!" Aidan reached down, unzipped his pants, pulled out a bag full of something that could have been meat, and tossed it to Frances McDormand, who was playing Stella.

Everybody laughed as she tried to catch the flying package, considering where it came from. The director said to Aidan, "You're not going to do that, are you?" Obviously, this wasn't his idea of Stanley, and it didn't make it into performance. Perhaps that was as it should be. But I thought it was a wonderful choice. Coming from Aidan's sense of humor, it seemed perfect for the character—he's crude but he's funny. And I am sure that it was essential that Aidan get that possibility out, whether it was used in the end or not. We have to respond personally to the script with whatever comes, no matter how foolish it is to others or even to us. The only rule is you must never physically hurt another actor or act out in a physically threatening way that enters into the other actor's space—touching or moving him—without having discussed and staged the physical encounter. That is not acceptable in class, rehearsal, or performance, no matter how much you may want to act on an aggressive impulse when you are in the moment.

When I find out what is not the character, everything else in me could be the character. So I'm free to do whatever I want until I find something else that is not the character. I am in a state of constant rehearsal, trying anything that comes to me. I'm not careful. In fact, the more arbitrary and outrageous I am, the better. If the choice doesn't work, it will be spectacularly apparent. And if it works, it will be simply spectacular.

When I go through a script with an actor, we take our time, stopping to talk about what each line means to the actor. I encourage, even push the actor to be inappropriate, to negate logic. I want him to go as far as possible. When Kevin Kline was exploring the role of Otto in *A Fish Called Wanda* with me, he had a line to Michael Palin the first time they meet: "That's some stutter."

I asked Kevin to stutter for me. I wanted to feel this and to respond for myself. As he stuttered, I found myself staring intently at his mouth. I was amazed and revolted at what was going on with his mouth and the sounds coming out of it. I found myself mimicking his stutter as he did it, mouthing the stutter, trying to guess the word he was so desperately trying to say. It was so cruel and so inappropriate! But we both realized at that moment, "Yes, that's Otto!"

Kevin kept up the process of exploration, making strong, even extreme choices when they came to him. When he was shooting the sex scene with Jamie Lee Curtis, he suddenly pulled off her knee-high boots, threw them off-camera, and sniffed his underarms to turn himself on. John Cleese, the writer and co-star, was standing next to the camera. He picked up one of the boots and threw it back to Kevin as the camera was rolling. Kevin grabbed the boot, put it to his face, and sniffed as if he were hyperventilating. It was an outrageous series of choices that just popped out of him. I guess Otto was talking to him—a dangerous thing. But no matter how stupid or bizarre, it was right, so right that it ranks right up there with his outrageous torture of Michael Palin by stuffing French fries up Palin's nose and eating his pet fish.

Again, you don't need to worry about consistency. Sometimes

an impulse that seems to contradict the rest of the characterization gives a performance a whole new depth and complexity. If an idea comes to you at a particular moment, don't reject it because it doesn't seem in keeping with how you've responded at other moments. Try it, and see if it works. This is another form of working from the negative.

In *Dangerous Liaisons*, Glenn Close plays the Marquise de Merteuil, a brilliant, powerful, dangerous aristocrat always in control, perfect and appropriate in appearance. Glenn's portrayal was steely, fierce, witty, contriving, sensual, and unmerciful. In the final scene, the Marquise wipes the make-up from her face while looking in the mirror. The shot is a harsh close-up, and Glenn let the moment into her. She didn't shy away from this terrifying shot, but instead revealed the pain of being battered by the lack of protection normally given to actresses—the soft lighting, perfect make-up, and loving camera angles that had made her so beautiful in *The Natural*. The depth of her vulnerability in this moment added a depth to the character we hadn't known was there, exposing the nakedness of the Marquise without her social status. We were forced to rethink the whole performance in relation to this moment. In theory, it might have seemed out of character for this intimidating woman, but in practice it was not. It was a brilliant choice.

Take the Script at Its Word

When the actor and I are first exploring the script together, I urge him to *take the lines literally*. Most actors don't believe the character is saying what he means. They immediately look for the subtext— what they think the character is really saying, below the surface of the line. I think that characters often mean exactly what they say, just as we do in life. And just as in life, the words may carry a subtext, which will resonate on its own if I mean exactly what I say. But if I try to *play* what I believe to be the subtext, I will spell out too much, giving the character away to the audience. Knowing too much, the audience will get bored. So will I. But playing what the character is literally saying can be very stimulating, allowing for lots of twists and turns moment by moment. Good dialogue partakes of the flux and irrationality of life, revealing ever-changing facets of the character.

For example, imagine I'm playing Willy Loman in Arthur Miller's *Death of a Salesman*. In the opening scene, I come into the kitchen late at night carrying two heavy suitcases. I put them down.

"Willy!" my wife, Linda, calls from the bedroom.

"It's all right," I say brightly. "I came back." I take these lines literally—it's no big deal.

"Why, what happened?" Linda says. "Did something happen, Willy?"

"No, nothing happened," I reassure her.

"You didn't smash the car, did you?" she asks, obviously worried.

"I said nothing happened." I feel angry at her assumption. "Didn't you hear me?" I bellow, thinking, Open your goddamn ears!

"Don't you feel well?" she says softly.

"I'm tired to death," I say quietly to myself, meaning it literally. I want to sleep forever and never wake up. I can't go on. Death is the only cure for how tired of life I am, I think.

I pause, realizing what I have just said. "I couldn't make it. I just couldn't make it, Linda," I admit to her, feeling so vulnerable, old, like a total failure.

"Where were you all day? You look terrible," she says.

She makes me laugh—her honesty, telling me how terrible I look.

"I got as far as a little above Yonkers," I answer lightly. "I stopped for a cup of coffee." I'm thinking, that's it. It must have been the coffee.

"What?" she asks.

"I suddenly couldn't drive any more," I explain. Of course, I had a bad reaction to the caffeine. It's that simple. "The car kept going off on to the shoulder." It was all because of the coffee!

"Oh, maybe it was the steering again," she says. "I don't think Angelo knows the Studebaker."

"No, it's me, it's me," I say, annoyed by her suggestion. I know it's not the mechanic's fault. "I realize I'm going sixty miles an hour and I don't remember the last five minutes. I'm—I can't seem to—keep my mind on it." I'm so angry at myself I want to scream. What's my damn problem?

"Maybe it's your glasses," she says, offering an explanation. "You never went for your new glasses."

"No, I see everything," I say, fed up with her patronizing. "I came back ten miles an hour. It took me nearly four hours," I spit out. Then I feel terrible about my crude behavior to Linda. She's just trying to make me feel better. Why am I getting angry at her?

You can see the twists and turns the lines inspire when I take them at face value, one by one. They stimulate my emotions and my imagination to go in many different directions, giving depth and texture to the performance.

Even a script that seems trivial may surprise us if we take it seriously. When I work with actors, I bring the same slow, patient exploration to an action movie as I would use with Shakespeare. The actor and I talk about what's going on in each scene, piece by piece, trying it out in many different ways. We don't set anything in the beginning, because we don't yet know what to hold on to, but we go as deeply as possible even if the script doesn't seem deep. The result can be a character with startling range and complexity, like Bridget Fonda's portrayal of Maggie in *Point of No Return*, or Mary Elizabeth Mastrantonio in *The Abyss*, or Aaliyah in *Romeo Must Die*.

The important thing is to take the time to explore as deeply and boldly as you can. Never skim. Leave no line of dialogue or moment unprobed. I don't want the actor to analyze, but that doesn't mean I don't want him to think about the character and the text. On the contrary, I want the actor obsessing passionately over the character and text. But I want him thinking about them in a way that isn't neat or tidy. I want him wandering around the character's dialogue, thoughts, feelings, and experiences.

Break the Rhythm

When Peter Fonda came to me in 1993, he wanted to rethink his acting. Early in his career he had a great success with *Easy Rider*, which he wrote and produced as well as starred in. He had been at the Actor's Studio and done many films but he thought it was time for some new input. For several years, we worked on lesser roles, in which he had been consistently doing very good work. Then one day he sent me a beautiful script, *Ulee's Gold*, the story of a bee-keeper who lives in Weewahatchee, Florida. He is a widower and has lost his son in Vietnam. His daughter returns home with her child in order to beat a drug habit, which brings a dangerous situation with it.

Peter had been moved to tears when he read the script. "I remember looking up at the ceiling of my log cabin and saying, 'I'd like to thank the members of the Academy . . . ' And my wife told me, 'Don't you ever tell anybody you said that.' " He'd been particularly struck by a description that read, "Ulee leaves the room with a gentle sorrow." Peter told me, "There is no book where I can go find what a gentle sorrow *is*. What does that mean? There's no dictionary for this kind of stuff." But the line had sparked something in him. He appeared in my living room, script in hand, and we went to work.

We started by taking the lines off the page, trying to uncover the character of Ulee. As Peter says, "What the actor reads on the page is totally different from what one speaks out in a story." He instinctively felt that it was a very special and quiet story that had to be played way down. "There were no dramatics thrown into it. Everything just flowed from the action," Peter recalls. "I realized the most important line in the film happens at the end. And it's not like the line from *Easy Rider*—'We blew it'—which is a major power line. This is a very simple line. Ulee says to one of the young punks, 'Meeting you, Eddie, has done me a world of good.' And Eddie says, 'How's that?' 'It reminds me that there's all kinds of weakness in the world, not all of it is evil. I forget that from time to time.' That was the heaviest line of the whole story and it was so beautifully written you didn't know it was the heaviest line. But for the character, it was."

Ulee's rhythms were entirely different from Peter's usual rhythms. Peter speaks quickly. His mind is running all the time, and he darts from one subject to another—"goes tangential," as he puts it. But Ulee had a cadence all his own. He was slow, grounded, of the earth. "He is a purposeful man who's led a very specific life in a very specific way," Peter puts it. "And he's forced to take a different course and become involved with others and make decisions that he thought he'd never have to make again."

Ulee began talking to Peter, and Peter listened to him while he took the lines off the page, keeping it slow, not needing to dramatize because "the words were very good," just improvising and letting the words take him. As Peter's rhythm of speaking changed, it affected him in profound ways. He found himself thinking differently, not only more slowly but more definitely, revealing a stolid, set character quite unlike his quicksilver, changeable, "tangential" self. This Peter was hidden yet transparent, hard yet sensitive, raging yet quiet. And all of this came to him early in our work together. Slowing his rhythm gave him the space to go down into himself and let the character talk to him. It freed him to be someone else so that he didn't have to Act. Instead, he showed up each day on the set and let himself go wherever the character took him, without losing confidence in himself. Once Ulee was talking to him, the rest was easy.

And eventually he found the "gentle sorrow" that had so moved him on first reading, letting it occur where it came to him, not where it was indicated in the script. Instead it happened earlier, when Patricia Richardson, who plays a nurse who rents a place across the street, comes in to talk to Ulee. Ulee offers her tea, and she accepts.

"She leaves the room and I'm there alone and I know what I have to do, we rehearsed it. I have to open a drawer, get a spoon, open a cupboard, get a cup and saucer. Get a paper napkin, put it down, take a teabag and put it in . . . Instead . . . well, I did that, but what happened is, I was liberated by this character, as an actor I was liberated. I opened the drawer and picked up the spoon; I looked at the spoon and if I paused at all it was a nanosecond of a pause but I thought, 'This is the first time I've used the real silver since Penelope died.' Penelope, my wife, was dead six years before the story starts. And then when I went up and reached out for a saucer and the cup—they weren't rigged, it was just my own natural shaking—it made a little noise and I thought to myself, 'This is the first time I've used the good china since Penelope died.' It's in that scene that there was a 'gentle sorrow.' "

Peter was just responding in the moment, allowing himself to react to what he was doing and saying. If he had forced the reaction, he "would have blown it totally." But it wasn't as if he was unaware of what was happening. "When I put the cup down, folded the napkin over, put the little silver teaspoon on the napkin, and then the teabag in the cup, I could hear all the women in the audience— 'Oh, look at that.' " And when they were shooting one of the bee-keeping scenes, he could hear some of the beekeepers' wives on the set whispering, "Oh, look, he's still wearing his wedding ring." "It meant something to them, and when I find those moments and feel them, I know that I hit it. It's the drug that makes me never want to stop doing this in my life. It's this wonderful feeling of—not escaping yourself but enlarging yourself, adding a character to yourself that's not you." Exploring the character with me, Peter found "the strength in Ulee's tenderness, rather than the weakness. [He] could find the strength in his quietness, rather than just withdrawal. [He] could find the strength that he didn't even know he had, until he was called upon to make very serious decisions."

It was a powerful performance unlike anything I had seen him do. The character of Ulee looked so natural that the audience could not see Peter acting and thought Peter Fonda must be just like Ulee. He isn't, and yet, paradoxically, Ulee was all Peter. Many in the film community were startled. Peter received a Golden Globe for best actor in a dramatic film and an Academy Award nomination for best actor. He received another Golden Globe and an Emmy Award the following year for his performance in *Ayn Rand*, in which he transformed himself richly and memorably into a man who is almost invisible.

Actors always ask me how to get to characters who are different from themselves. Well, every character has to be us, or they won't be believable. We will look like we are Acting. But getting to characters that seem different from us and yet believable and interesting is necessary for us to fulfill our potential as actors.

In order to do this we have to throw ourselves into unfamiliar, even uncomfortable, rhythms that actually make us *feel* different. When I negate an actor's normal rhythm and push him into new and unknown cadences, he finds aspects within himself that he didn't realize were there. And yet these aspects turn out to be familiar—like opening yourself to another you living within you.

The actor has to re-create himself every time out, with each role. He has to have the courage to start work on a new character as if he knows nothing about the character, nothing about himself—and nothing about acting. He has to accept the fact that he doesn't know where he is going to go with a new script or how he is going to discover and play a new character. To discard old patterns of acting and tricks, he must break his usual rhythms of talking and physicalizing.

If I'm working on a new script with an actor I know well, I try to help him discover a rhythm different from his natural rhythm and different from other roles he has played. I do this by consciously taking him away from what is comfortable. I distance him from what he knows too well. Once again, I work from the negative.

Ally Sheedy is a very energetic person. She speaks fast and is passionate about things. She's never laid back, and it's impossible for her to hide her feelings.

When she took on the part of Lucy in the film *High Art*, it was obvious that Ally's usual rhythms wouldn't work. In the film, a young editor new to photo publishing convinces Lucy to do a layout for her magazine. The two develop a sexual relationship in the process, which complicates both lives. Lucy is a photographer whose work is recording her own life as part of a counterculture of artists and drug addicts. She dropped out of the fast-moving art world after a book of her photography was a great success. She is secretive, mysterious. We can discern what she's feeling only if we look hard. She's always thinking, but we never know what. Lucy is totally hidden.

I encouraged Ally to open herself to a rhythm completely different from her natural one. We started by taking the lines off the page, emphasizing the character's quiet, her stillness. After all, we reasoned, a photographer is an observer. And since her subject is her own life, we figured she'd be quiet in order to observe, but not disturb, whatever she was photographing. Even the camera she uses, an old Leica, is quiet. And the heroin Lucy uses stills her and slows her body's rhythms.

This process of exploration carried over to the set. Ally recalls, "To be in a scene and do absolutely nothing, that took a lot of courage. You think, I should be interesting." But she allowed herself "just to do nothing except think whatever I was thinking and not say the line until I was ready."

In the film there's a moment when the young woman knocks on Lucy's door. Lucy opens the door and leans against it, looking directly at the girl as if studying her face. She says nothing. It's as if, even though she isn't holding a camera, she's composing a photograph of this chatty young woman. Ally's stillness is so full that in a couple of seconds the girl is a wreck. She can't do anything until Lucy finally invites her in.

"For Lucy," Ally said to me, "this girl at that moment is the door back into some kind of life." That's what Ally was thinking about as she watched this girl in the doorway. "Do I want to go back into life?" Ally had an understanding of what it means to be an artist who leaves a big-time career to avoid the unpleasant demands of fame and doesn't want to go back—or is at least unsure. "I was at a point where I was working a lot and had a lot of success at a young age," Ally told me. "Then it got very directionless. I wanted things that were much more complicated and much more interesting—not just movies and being a star. I was very frustrated. I felt like I was going on this downhill slide." So she came back to New York City where she could continue studying as well as act off Broadway and in small independent films. Ally didn't drop out as Lucy did, but she empathized with Lucy's discontent.

Ally won an Independent Film Spirit Award for her portrayal of Lucy and allowed audiences to rediscover her as an actor. If they assumed she is like Lucy, they were wrong. But Ally understood Lucy. More important, she forced herself to drop her own natural rhythms and find Lucy's, inhabiting the character so completely that no one could see her acting.

It's a curious thing that when we approach a new character, we think that we will naturally shift to different rhythms. But the truth is that we often don't, because we are afraid to let go of what we think has been working for us. This gets more difficult as actors have more success because they are often given what seems like the same role again and again. *But each character is different.* We have to discover the difference by breaking our comfortable rhythms and discovering a new rhythm for this particular character. And we often have to do this consciously.

This is a particularly big problem for actors who have found success on television as a continuing character. Take Candice Bergen, with whom I worked on the pilot for *Murphy Brown.* With that part, she found a character whose rhythm was totally different from her natural rhythm. And then she played Murphy for nine seasons, winning countless awards.

After the series ended, she was asked to do a film in which her character was nothing like Murphy Brown. When we worked together, it took a great deal of effort to get Murphy's rhythm out of Candice. She was so comfortable in the familiar groove that she automatically went there. Candice is smart and a good actress, so she knew that Murphy's way of speaking was wrong for this new character. But at first she couldn't shake it. So we took the character's lines off the page together, consciously rejecting the old rhythms. She started to find a new rhythm that came from within the dialogue of the character we were working on—a subtle, sensitive, lonely woman who falls in love with a mildly retarded young man. Candice gradually changed her vocal patterns, rejecting the first music of a phrase in her mouth. Instead of going up, she'd go down. Eventually, she uncovered the character. Her emotions were free again to respond to what she said.

We have worked on several films since that one, and in each, Murphy has receded more and more. But nine years is a long time with one character, and we often joke that Murphy is always lurking somewhere in Candice, just waiting to break out.

Similarly, Bruce Willis came to me many years ago to work on an audition for the leading role in a film called *In Country*. He had already enjoyed great success with the television series *Moonlighting*, and then with *Die Hard*. But the character in this new film couldn't have been farther from what he had been playing. The character was a Vietnam veteran plagued by combat flashbacks who was having trouble reentering civilian life. His language was not facile. His relationships were complicated in a silent way. He feared what was within him.

When Bruce and I began reading the new script together, it became immediately apparent that his rhythm with the dialogue was too light, too easy, for this troubled character. I pressed him to take the lines off the page piece by piece—to take his time, breathe, let the material take him wherever it went. He is a very good and experienced actor, and he understood what I meant. But no sooner did he start to do as I asked then he'd slip back into his more familiar way of handling lines. He knew it was wrong for this character. But after many years of success on TV and in films, it was not easy to drop it.

For three hours we took the dialogue off the page while I repeated again and again, "Too much. Just say it." We worked until there wasn't a trace of *Moonlighting* left. His rhythm was totally different. His pitch was different. His thinking was different. The character was in a deep well and Bruce dived down into himself to find him. At the end, he said, "I got it, Harold. I understand." And he did. He auditioned for the director, got the part, and received serious respect for a deep, powerful portrayal that was different from his previous parts. The key was breaking a rhythm that he didn't realize was so much a part of his acting.

Let the Script Guide the Research

As I have said, I am not opposed to research in the process of an actor's work on character. Research is often necessary to teach us specific things we must know because they're what the character knows. But the actor must use his research to broaden his exploration, not limit his instinct and imagination. Research should be used judiciously, and the actor should rely on the script to guide him. The script tells us what research we need and also when to give it up and trust the text. Otherwise our research can swamp the character, obscuring our sense of his specific nature.

When Matt Dillon first came to work with me it was for *Drugstore Cowboy*. His character was Bob Hughes, "really an interesting character," Matt remembers. "The guy was such a determined kind of hard-core dope fiend. He was myopic in his search for drugs. So I really got into it. It lent itself to research." A friend of Matt's was a recovering addict. "We went around together. I met him in the East Village at a club—a ground zero for addicts who spent maybe two hours a day sober. So they had no time to worry about being clean. You could see people with open abscesses in shooting galleries. We'd meet guys in wheelchairs selling their syringes, guys with diabetes. There was something very sad about a lot of these people."

But as we explored the script, the "feeling of darkness" these field trips inspired felt different from what the script suggested. The characters were "like Bonnie and Clyde. They were professional criminals. It was a gang. And that was different." The script had a lot of long dialogues, and I sensed Matt's frustration that he was playing it all so dark, so heavy.

I suggested taking it in another direction. I wanted Matt to forget about his research and let the dialogue play on him, so that moment by moment he could let in a lighter side of himself. I suggested he think of it more like a comedy.

"It was a great suggestion," Matt remembers. "In actuality there was a real playfulness with this character. There was a sense of *I Love Lucy* or *The Honeymooners*—these two couples bickering all the time as they go around the country robbing pharmacies."

Piece by piece, we pulled the long stretches of dialogue off the page. Matt started to let go, and his wit and intelligence brought a charm to the character that played as a counterpoint to the dark aspects of the addict's life. This allowed not only Matt but the character to be aware of the absurdity of his life. No longer overwhelmed by his research, Matt was able to conceive of the character apart from the drugs. The character surfaced in him—a very specific person capable of loving and living another kind of life. The character became accessible to us—even attractive. We could see why he was the leader of this ragtag gang of outlaws roaming the countryside, breaking into drugstores. They weren't just "sniveling junkies." We liked them, and him, yet we never stopped believing for a moment that he was a drug addict—a troubled, flawed character.

Once Matt made contact with the character, he was able to use his research. "My friend told me stories, like one time when he was making dinner for his wife and while he was cooking the fish and the vegetables, he thought, I'll just take a quick shot of dope. He nods out and when she comes back the whole kitchen is on fire and they're beating the shit out of each other." In the end, Matt used his research to inform the character without overwhelming the character's specific qualities.

In *Single White Female*, Jennifer Jason Leigh played a psychotic character who systematically takes over her roommate's life. I was afraid that Jennifer's research on psychosis, although comprehensive and very good, was preventing her from letting herself into the character.

"That was a great note for me," Jennifer recalls. "There's a tremendous strength and confidence you get from distancing yourself from the character through all that research. So to have you—someone I really trust—gently say to me, 'Just be careful and bring yourself into it because you're verging on dangerous territory'—made me feel like I was being brought into a safe place—*not* being cut off, and *not* being judged for it. And so I still felt free to use everything I had done. It wasn't like you were saying, throw away this research, it's not good. You were saying just be careful and bring yourself into it."

Jennifer's performance was startling, frightening, and totally believable. Her research was there, but so was she. And so the character was very personal, very human.

The creative process necessitates giving up normal logic. We have to be in a trial-and-error state where unlikely connections can be made. Creativity occurs when things that don't seem to belong together make something new when joined. It's what I call the "illogical conclusion." That's what we want in our acting—characters who are not just recognizable but surprising, unexpected, stimulating.

Kevin Kline once told me, "What I learned from you was to create characters whose nature gave me the freedom to do whatever I wanted. And the more complete the characterization, the more complete the freedom." Maybe that's part of the trick—to conceive characters who are not just believable but whom the actor feels free playing.

I know the process of getting there takes patience, bravery, and concentration. Don't rush it. If you have the courage to take your time at the beginning, you will find that the rest of the process goes much faster. Obstacles always come up, both practical and psychological. That's what the rest of this book is about—the specific problems actors face while they are trying to do their best. But when you have given yourself a thorough, leisurely start exploring the character, you will not feel rushed in the rehearsal process in the theater, or in the shooting process in film. On the contrary, you will feel a certain confidence at having given yourself the luxury of taking it slowly. And best of all, you will feel the joy and exhilaration of going out on a limb.

Suggestions for Practice

Trace the character of Irina or Andrei in Chekhov's *The Three Sisters* through the whole play.

Start by taking all of Irina's or Andrei's lines off the page as you read through the play from beginning to end. Then, as you are reading, pick several important moments in the play to work on in depth. Try to condense the lines into a monologue.

For the women, for instance, if you are exploring Irina, start with two of the monologues I suggested in chapter 1. Begin with the first scene in Act I—"Tell me why am I so happy?"—and continue with her lines through "I am twenty years old!" cutting out Chebutykin's and Olga's few lines. At this point in the play everything is hopeful for Irina—it's her birthday and the first anniversary of her father's death so the mourning period has ended. She wakes up believing she finally knows what she wants and what is important in her life: "Man must work by the sweat of his brow." She is young, naïve, and full of energy.

Then, when Irina enters in Act II, a couple of years have passed. String her lines together beginning with "How tired I am" and ending at "almost a year," cutting Tuzenbach's and Masha's lines. In this scene she admits how hateful and boring her work in the telegraph office is. "It's work without poetry, without meaning." She tells of being cruel to a distressed woman. "I was rude to her for no reason. I haven't got the time, I said."

In Act III, begin with "Yes, how shallow our Andrei has become . . . ," stringing Irina's lines together as a monologue that ends with "But it all turned out to be foolishness." This moment when Irina is so unhappy that she can no longer imagine going on any longer—"Turn me out, turn me out"—is a kind of breakdown for Irina, her low point in the play: "Life is slipping by, never to return."

In Act IV attach the speech starting with Irina's line to Kulygin, "If only you knew how hard it has been to live here alone . . . " to her scene with Tuzenbach when she says, "I have never in my life been in love. Oh, how I have dreamed of love, dreamed of it for a long time now, day and night, but my soul is like a fine piano that is locked and the key lost." Within this monologue, Irina moves from disappointment, to hope, to despair.

For the men working on Andrei in *The Three Sisters*, start with Act I, "Come, that's enough," and after cutting Vershinin's lines continue to "But what a cost!" This short monologue introduces Andrei's complex feelings about his father and his studies. Then create another short monologue revealing his desire for real love by stringing together his lines from his scene with Natasha, starting with "My darling, I beg of you . . ." to "I love you, love you, as I have never loved anyone before."

Then, in Act II, a few years later, piece together from Andrei's scene with Ferapont an unusual and important monologue about Andrei's present disappointment with his work and his desire for the life of a scholar in Moscow. Start with "Tomorrow is Friday," cut Ferapont's lines, and continue with Andrei's lines until "A stranger and lonely."

In Act III, Andrei's monologue to his sisters, who are hidden from his view behind screens, begins with "I'll just say it and then go." Cut Kulygin's line and then continue until "My dear sisters, my darling sisters, don't believe me, don't believe me." In this monologue Andrei hears things coming out of his mouth that after a point he has to admit are lies. This is the most important moment in the play for him.

In Act IV, string together a monologue starting with Andrei's line to Chebutykin "A wife is a wife . . ." through "I don't understand why, for what reason, I love her so, or at least, did love her." Then add Andrei's lines with Ferapont from "Oh. Where is it, where has it all gone, when I was young, gay, clever . . ." to " . . . they become the same pitiful, identical corpses as their fathers and mothers." This monologue completes the path of the character in the play.

Working this way traces much of what the character is, and will allow an actor to explore the complications of the character in a way that is not so different from rehearsing a play for performance.

Remember to start by taking all the character's lines off the page while reading the play from beginning to end. Then, while continuing to reread the play a number of times, work in depth on each of these monologues. At first, do the monologues in sequence to feel the flow of the character within your responses. Then work on each monologue in depth for a few days. Work until the lines start coming to you without looking down. But *don't memorize*! Let them memorize themselves. Then go on to the next monologue and the next. Finally, do all the monologues in sequence in one sitting. Try this for several days.

Don't hold on to your choices even if they are working. Keep exploring new possibilities for the character and you. Remember to go to the negative when you are bored, know too much about how the character should be played, or are stuck. Or try the five different ways mentioned on page 30. Force yourself to take chances and keep exploring.

If you want to work with a partner, try the characters of Paul and Susan in Michael Weller's *Loose Ends*. Start by taking all of your character's lines off the page as you read the whole play. In Scene 1 start at the beginning, which includes the monologues mentioned on pages 32–34. Now use them in the scene together with your partner. Continue with the scene until Paul's line, "I don't believe this is really happening. I really don't." This is the beginning of their relationship.

Then work on Paul and Susan in scene 5 starting with Susan's line, "Want some more?" Continue to the end of the scene. This is an important point in the play where they have been apart and meet again.

Follow this with Scene 7 from Paul's line, "I should explain this . . . " to the end of the scene. Cut Ben's lines and Susan's lines from "Would you leave us alone" to "All of you please." Also cut Ben's interruption and Paul's response. You will find this is a huge complicated scene, full of rage, pain, love, and loss. When pieced together with the earlier scenes, it will help you to discover your-self in these characters.

Add any other scenes you may be excited to work on. Go back over the whole play a number of times, taking your character's lines off the page. Don't set anything in stone, but accept and trust those things that do come back again and again. That's what happens when you become the character.

Try this approach with many different plays, working alone and with a partner. *Work every day on your acting*. This means verbalizing lines every day, *not* just thinking about the character. The actor's work is always connected to the text. You will find that the more you trust yourself when verbalizing a line, with no preconceptions or control, the freer you will find yourself when you are on stage or in front of a camera with no lines to say—the more life you will have in the moment.

3

I WANT THIS PART. HOW CAN I GET IT?

"I have always felt that if I go in and do what I feel is my best, then I don't care if I'm not cast, because then I'm just not what they're looking for. But if I go in and for one reason or another do not do my best, that hurts."

—Glenn Close

Glenn Close hated to audition. When she first came to see me, in fact, she'd just had an audition, for The Manhattan Theater Club's production of *The Singular Life of Albert Knobbs*—"a wonderful play," she recalls. She was intrigued by the part of Albert Knobbs, a subtle and complex woman who had lived her life as a man. But auditioning made no sense to Glenn: "You go in and you read for five minutes, and that's it. I started reading and I stopped and said, 'You know what? I'm wasting my time and I'm wasting your time. And so, good-bye.' "

That was not the end of the story, however. "It turned out that the fact that I had stopped and excused myself was the most interesting thing that had happened in the audition all day," Glenn continues. "So they asked me to come back, but I didn't want to go back until I really knew what I was going to do." Glenn called

Kevin Kline and he gave her my name. And when she came in to see me, she said, "I want this part. How can I get it?"

We had barely started reading together when Glenn suddenly began to weep, and then she lifted the script over her head with both hands and let it fly. I ducked reflexively, but it landed on the floor just a few feet from where she was seated. Although Glenn has no recollection of this, I do—it was so vivid. But she does recall how frustrated she was: "I was tired of feeling vulnerable not knowing how to approach auditions. And I had been acting for a number of years."

She was desperately trying to get into the character of Albert Knobbs. Like most actors, she had difficulty breaking through the barrier of shyness when encountering a new role, as she describes in chapter 1, and she needed long periods of rehearsal to build her portrayal. But there is little time to prepare for auditions in theater or film, and in the audition itself, the actor has only one or two scenes to define the character.

When Glenn pulled herself together, we got to work. I told her to take the time to take it off the page. "Just that," she says, "was major," a way to avoid being in "this deer in the headlights situation where you don't breathe and you're not letting yourself be aware of the world around you." We went through the script phrase by phrase, thought by thought, image by image for several hours that evening. Her work started to have a calmness and a freedom that hadn't been there before. Her emotions were full. The lines were affecting her in a very subtle and personal way. She was truly beginning to find the character hidden within—a character whose real identity as a woman was not discovered until her death.

But this was just the beginning of the character work. What to do about the audition the next day?

I said, "Do the same thing. Take it off the page for them. Don't worry about what comes out. It doesn't have to be the same things that happened tonight. The lines and images may affect you differently tomorrow. Let it go wherever it goes. Most important, let them see you exploring right in front of them, without any care about whether your responses are right or wrong. Forget about performing for them. Let them see how you work, what makes you tick. Then they will get glimpses of your real response to this character and why they will need what you have to offer."

A few days later, Glenn called to tell me she got the part. She had approached the audition in an entirely new way. Instead of thinking about what she should or could do, she had taken the time to explore the text, doing what interested *her* with each line, each moment.

Having landed the part, Glenn came back to work through the character of Albert Knobbs with me. She won an Obie Award for her portrayal, and over the next decade we worked together on almost all of her roles in film and theater, up through *Fatal Attraction*. She never went back to her old way of auditioning because she had come to a crucial insight: "It's insane to go in and think you're going to give a performance." Instead, she said, "You come in with your own calm agenda, which is, I'll see what I can do. All of a sudden you're doing it on your own terms. It was from that moment that I was able to go on auditions and say, 'You know what? I'm just going to throw out a couple of ideas,' rather than saying, 'This is going to be my performance.' " Freed from the pressure to perform, she could respond to her own and other characters' lines with instinct and immediacy, revealing herself and the possibilities she offered for the character much more fully. And that is the best we have as actors.

Most actors are plagued by auditions, especially at the beginning of their careers. This chapter is about how to deal with the problems actors face at auditions, and a healthy way to think about the process. Much of what I believe and recommend runs contrary to the general thinking on the subject. But over the years I have had a great deal of success helping actors prepare for auditions—inexperienced young actors as well as major established actors.

My fundamental belief is this: auditioning is the beginning of the actor's work on character—a free, responsive exploration that allows the director or casting director to see the instinctive connections between the actor and the character. Performance is an informed exploration an audience sees after a long, in-depth exploration by the actor in rehearsal.

When you're performing, you may think you have a road map—and you'll have to get rid of it if you want to be any good. When you're auditioning, you know you don't have a road map. It's too early to even pretend that you do. You are roaming around a new country, and if you see a road that looks interesting, you must have the courage and curiosity to take it, without worrying whether it's a dead end. If the actor stops thinking that he can actually give a performance in an audition, his wide-open exploration can be very revealing both to him and to those who are watching, offering insights into the character they didn't expect. But first he has to be armed with a few do's and don'ts to overcome the obstacles to this freedom.

Ignore the Casting Description

Casting is a chemical thing: directors and casting directors have an instinct for it, just as actors have an instinct for acting. They may think they know what they want, but a casting description means nothing once they watch a real actor work in front of them. At that moment they are simply responding, and they can't control their responses. They can intellectualize about what they saw after the fact, but the response itself is pretty much everything.

It is necessary for the actor to *allow this response*. The more the actor tells them about the character, and the harder he tries to act the ideas spelled out in the casting description, the less opportunity the observers have to react. When every actor is going for the same thing, and the casting directors can see it coming, they get bored. What they really need is to be surprised. They need to discover the actor right there in the audition.

In order for this to happen, the actor must be open and responsive to the material—that is, to the script and the dialogue as they affect him moment by moment. Since it is the beginning of his work on the character, the fewer decisions he makes in advance, the more possibilities there are to surprise himself and the observers.

The hardest part of auditioning is being free enough not to care where you're going with the character or scene, so that those for whom you're auditioning get a chance to see you exploring in front of them. Exploration is more attractive, revealing, and useful than anything else you can do. But the actor often serves as his own worst enemy at the audition by caring too much about the casting director's description of what he thinks the director wants, the director's idea of what he's looking for, and the actor's own conception of what the character is supposed to be.

Don't look for right choices. Do what interests you and what you really believe at that moment, because that is the best you have to offer. An audition is about letting them see who you are, how you work, and how the material affects you. An audition should be as much for you as for them.

Don't Memorize

I believe it is better not to memorize the lines for an audition. I know this is not the general view, but I think memorizing lines creates an added concern—you'll be afraid that you will forget them. You should always have the script open and in front of you. If you really know a line, then say it. Otherwise, just look down and take it off the page.

I'll go further: you should *never* try to memorize anything!

If you are working correctly, you will come to know your lines simply by listening to the other characters and responding. If you spend as much time as I am asking you to spend on taking it off the page, you'll find you memorize the lines without being aware of it. Even long monologues come naturally and easily this way, because the thoughts and images in your head are coming from the lines you've taken off the page. There's nothing, therefore, to forget.

Prepare for Auditions by Taking the Other Characters' Lines Off the Page

When you prepare for an audition, take the other characters' lines off the page as well as your own. By this I mean make their lines what you are hearing or what you are thinking about. Say them out loud. Improvise with them. Free-associate with them. Verbalize your thoughts and feelings about them. In fact, spend more time on the other characters' lines. Make them yours.

Working this way forces you to listen and to be available when auditioning and acting, instead of overworking your lines. By taking your attention off yourself and how you're going to say your next line, you will be ready to focus on the reader and, most important, what he's saying to you. How your line comes out is then a surprise. This is the beginning of real freedom in acting.

Suppose I am preparing to audition for the role of Medvedenko, the schoolteacher in Chekhov's *The Seagull*, and I'm preparing the opening scene we discussed in chapter 1. I start with my first line: "Why do you always wear black?" I breathe in and out, letting the question roll around in my head and then look up and say the line out loud for myself.

Then I look down at the next line. It is Masha's: "I am in mourning for my life." I take her line off the page, as I did mine. I breathe in and out, look up, and say it. Then I repeat it, making it mine: "You're in mourning for your life?" I think, You believe your life is over? Why? I let her line wander around in my thoughts as long as it interests me. I think, What an over-dramatic load of crap! I may even verbalize it. Then I look down for her next line, "I am unhappy." I repeat the process. I say, "You're unhappy?" And then I verbalize my thought: "What do you have to be unhappy about?" I look down at my next line, "Why? I don't understand . . . " I look up and say it for myself. Looking down I read, "You are in good health." I look up and say it, feeling irritated with her. "I'm the one who should be unhappy," I say. She's healthy! And so on and on.

I repeat this for the remainder of the scene, taking the time to verbalize Masha's lines and my thoughts about what she means. I spend more time on her lines than on Medevenko's. This puts me in a responsive state with her lines, almost like listening. Spending so much time dealing with her lines and my feelings about them helps my own lines come to me easily and allows me to explore. Things become apparent to me about the scene but I make no hard decisions. If an idea strikes me, I make myself available to it. I don't force myself to repeat it. In fact, each time I take my lines and the other character's lines off the page, I let them go wherever they go. Sometimes I do something outrageous—yell when I'm saying something sweet, or do something stupid that doesn't make sense, or gently say something that is really cruel—to allow myself to be arbitrary. In this way, I explore my lines and the other character's lines in many different ways, opening myself to a range of possibilities.

Dress to Feel the Part, Not to Look the Part

Often actors dress to show the director what they think the character should look like. But if you are too specific about look or dress, you may shortchange yourself and the character. You must remember that you don't know this character yet; you are just beginning to explore. And there is nothing more disconcerting than seeing an actor come into an audition in costume and make-up. It seems desperate and amateurish; it doesn't allow the auditors room to respond.

So don't think about the look of the character. Instead, wear whatever makes it easiest for you to feel comfortable with the character's words and lines. Let the character tell you what to wear or what not to wear. Dress for yourself, not for the audience. If you think you should be sexy, dress to feel sexy, not to look sexy. Trust your instinct.

Don't Work Yourself into an Emotional State

It is not uncommon to enter the waiting area for an audition and see actors who won't talk to or look at anyone else. They have worked themselves up into what they think is the requisite emotional state for the audition and are desperately trying to hold on to it while they go over and over their lines.

This is not a good idea, because when the actor comes to audition, he may find himself waiting a very long time before he gets his chance to be seen. As the actor waits, that edge of concentration will drain out of him. When he is finally called, he won't be able to listen or respond, for fear of losing what remains of his keyed-up energy. Working for the emotion, he will miss being truthfully in the moment.

Don't work yourself into an emotional state, because in the end, the emotion will be too forced. Trust yourself, and stay in the moment. As Glenn Close says so perfectly, "That's basically the strongest thing you can show: that you hear, you respond, and you take your time to show there's something going on between your ears."

Note: You may find the section on "Getting to Big Emotional Moments" in chapter 5 useful for auditioning as well.

Come with Your Own Agenda

Arrive at the audition with ideas or choices—just a few of them—that interest you. The more things that interest you, the merrier—but don't set them in stone. Come prepared to play with them. Then you will be open to your responses in the audition room, and new choices may arise instinctively.

I remember an audition for the Gravedigger in *Hamlet* at the Public Theater. Kevin Kline was to play Hamlet, and he didn't like the candidates for the role that he'd seen in the director's casting sessions. He called and asked me to read. I usually like to be outside productions my clients are involved with, but in this case I figured, what the hell.

I had only a day to prepare. As I was exploring the scene on my own, taking the lines into myself and verbalizing them, I instinctively thought, "Don't try to be funny, but allow yourself to be irreverent." Even though I knew the play very well, I had never worked on the Gravedigger except to read opposite Kevin in coaching sessions. So for me, it was like beginning on a new character.

I thought, I'm a gravedigger. Every day a new body. Every time I dig a grave, another bone. Shovel them in, day in, day out. It's all work to me. As I explored the lines over and over in the short time I had, I kept going to different places, sometimes bored, sometimes playful, mean, angry, clever, stupid—but interestingly, *always* uncaring.

I thought, like all work, digging graves is probably boring. So I have to amuse myself. But how to keep myself interested? As I let the lines wash over me, I realized that the Gravedigger is messing with people all the time. For example, he mocks the coroner's decision not to say that Ophelia drowned herself, in order to allow her a Christian burial. "Here lies the water—good. Here stands the man—good. If the man go to this water and drown himself, it is will he nil he goes—mark you that. But if the water come to him and drown him, he drowns not himself. Argal, he that is not guilty of his own death shortens not his own life."

Everyone else is spooked by graveyards and death, but to the Gravedigger, they're a job, so he sings while digging.

HAMLET. Has this fellow no feeling of his business? 'A sings in grave-making?

HORATIO. Custom hath made it in him a property of easiness.

HAMLET. 'Tis e'en so, the hand of little employment hath the daintier sense.

At the audition, I was singing very loudly and badly in the grave (I'm a terrible singer, but it's fun to make people cringe) when I heard these lines. I thought, Here's a "dainty sense"— Kevin—to play with. In the script, my direction is "Throws up a skull." I threw my book at Kevin. He was surprised and bobbled it. I grabbed the book back, looked down at the line, then looked up and said, "That skull had a tongue in it, and could sing once." A lot better than me, I thought, smiling. Everyone laughed.

I hadn't planned to do these things. But when I came into the audition, I could see that Kevin was somewhat uncomfortable with me there. I was letting him know that anything was possible, that he'd better stay on his toes with me. This choice came, like everything else that day, from my improvisation on the text, my personal response to everything playing on me in the moment, and a few ideas that interested me while "preparing." I didn't know ahead of time just what I was going to do, so everything was fresh.

Kevin called to tell me how startled he had been, and how refreshing it was. And I was called back. At the call-back, though, the director started to direct me, and I saw that he had a different vision of the character. It was a legitimate truth about the character, but it didn't interest me. I tried pieces of it on for size, to see how it fit, and then went back to letting myself wander through the scenes. He cast someone else in the part, and when I saw the production, it was clear to me that what he wanted wasn't something I could have given authentically. Even if I had managed to tailor myself to look like what he wanted in the audition, I wouldn't have had a good experience acting in the production, and he wouldn't have liked what he got.

Give Them Many Choices

The key to auditioning is to separate yourself from the crowd—to give the observers many choices, instead of trying to please the director by guessing which one he wants. Remember, the actor who only concerns himself with being free and available to his responses is the actor who will be watched.

Directors like to direct. They are more than ready to offer direction if you are interesting, even if you're making a different choice from what they want. But you won't be interesting if you're not free. If the director suggests something, give it a try. But also keep exploring the places that are fresh for you. You have to go lots of places in order to find the best one. But even if only one of the choices you make works, the director will see it, and that's what he'll remember.

What do you do if the direction you're getting doesn't make sense to you? Just go somewhere other than where you went before. What you just did didn't work for the director, or he wouldn't be offering direction. So whatever you did before, *don't* do again. Do something else, even the opposite of what you did. But do it consciously only for the first line or so. After that, take a breath and go wherever you want—explore. An actor can do almost anything well for a line or two. After that, you've got to be totally free in order to be good. Directors will recognize and appreciate your freedom. They may even think the difference in your work was triggered by their suggestions. And in a way it is.

Just remember: exploration equals freedom. So don't try to please them.

Do Only One Thing at a Time

If you are reading, you can't be talking. If you are talking or listening, you shouldn't be reading. You can't access a complete range of responses if part of your mind is reading while your mouth is moving, or while the other actor or the casting director is talking to you. When I'm preparing an actor for an audition, I sit across the room from him taking the lines off the page in the same way I'm asking the actor to take it off the page. When the actor is saying his line, I look at him and listen. I'll know when I have a line. The actor will stop talking, or something will prompt me to look down.

Even more importantly, I don't care what my next line is. Sneaking a look at it while the actor is saying his would only take me away from my responses—away from my feelings and instinct. I need to listen, or I have no real response. I let my response to the actor's line take me wherever it goes. I never know where I'm going and I don't care. Then I look down and pull up my line. My response to it may take me someplace unexpected. I let that happen because it's interesting to me, to the actor opposite me, and in an audition, to those watching. That's because it's surprising. And my response is real.

So while the casting director is reading, don't read his line or your line. Just listen. When he stops—then and only then—look down and get your line. Then look up and say it. Feel free to blurt it out any way it comes.

I had an audition for a small part in a Sidney Lumet film many years ago. I first read for the casting director. She said her line, and I just looked at her, because her head was in the page. There was a silence, and then she looked up. Then I looked down, picked up my line, looked up, and said it. She was now watching me as I spoke. She was not reading my line as I was saying it. We went on like this, with her looking up at me each time.

She must have been pleased, because even though I was much too young for the role, she sent me on to read for Lumet. He also read with me. Predictably, his head was down in the page. I did the same thing I'd done with the casting director. I waited for him to look up from the page. Then I looked down and got my line, looked up, and said it with him looking at me. He smiled and we went on like this.

When we finished, the first thing he said was, "Harold, tell me about yourself. Who did you study acting with?"

I didn't get the part. But the director was engaged by me and therefore was curious about who I was, where I came from, what my acting was about. That is all we can ask from an audition—the auditor's engagement with us. That way, they don't forget us.

Many actors are afraid that working this way will leave too many pauses. So what? What's the rush? Besides, they're not stupid out there. They see the actor look down to get the line. So of course there's a bit of a pause. They know this script is new to you and that you are at the beginning of your work on the character.

And think of this: what they see when you are listening is you. And what they see when you are talking is you, not some actor with his head buried in the page, reading, waiting for his cue, approximating the way the line should sound—in other words, giving a line reading. That's the best he can do, because operating this way, he doesn't have a real response. Why? Because he wasn't listening. He was worrying about not leaving pauses. This is of no use to those watching. It tells them nothing about the actor.

What do you do if the director or the casting director asks you to go faster?

Here's a simple trick. Pick up the cue for the first line you say. Pounce on your line without questioning it at all. Or tie your first two lines of dialogue together so they move quickly. Take a pause and breathe. Then go back to taking it off the page. This will satisfy the director because you can do that for a moment—for a line or two—without being false or boring. Any longer and your responses will become generalized, which leads to repetition and dullness. You will not be responding to what you are hearing or reading. You will be thinking about going fast.

Work with What the Reader Gives You

Actors often come back from auditions and complain to me, "When you are acting opposite me, I'm alive and free, because you are a good actor. You're giving me something to respond to. In the audition the reader was bad. I didn't get anything from him."

I say, "Thank you very much, but that's not true. You were getting the most important thing from the reader—the line!" It doesn't matter how badly the line is read. If the actor is listening and not reading, the lines will mean something to him. He will have a real response. And so he will have something to say with his line. In fact, a strange delivery from a reader may create new feelings about the lines—feelings the actor didn't expect.

The director and casting director hear the reader's line as well as the lines from the actor auditioning. But they are only interested in the actor and his response. If he is alive and listening when someone else is talking as well as when he is talking, that doubles their pleasure.

Attack Your Fear

Fear is a big subject in acting. It is always with us, no matter how experienced we are. At the beginning of our careers, we're afraid of being untalented, unprofessional, forgettable, or just plain bad. Later we fear being disappointing and undeserving of our success. But there is nothing more consistently frightening than auditioning for a role. After all, everyone is afraid of talking in front of strangers, especially strangers who are judging us.

Unfortunately, fear is one feeling we can't use in acting because it incapacitates us. Fear weakens the actor, undermining his trust in himself and his instinct. Fear keeps him from taking chances, from being foolish and risking failure. Failure is not what we think—failing to get the part. Failure is being dull! So to give in to fear by hiding behind preparation or technique makes no sense in acting. When we are acting, we are already in an exposed place. Everything we do is visible to those watching—they can see our fear, they can see us hiding, they can see our timidity. They may understand it and recognize the reasons for it, but they will not accept it, because our job as actors is to surprise them, to interest them, to startle them. There is no place to hide.

If you walk into an audition prepared with every choice spelled out you will have to fulfill all those choices. In the tense atmosphere of an audition this obligation will increase your fear and deaden both your instinct and feelings.

The best way to deal with your fear is to attack it. For instance, if when you come into the audition room you are afraid to take your time, take a long pause at the very start. Don't say your line. Let the silence make the reader and anyone else in the room look up and stop what they're doing. Then take a breath and begin.

By waiting, you will have challenged your fear. At first you will feel the fear intensify. But then it will dissipate, leaving you feeling strong and free to do what you want. Usually actors don't take time. They think they want to get it over with. But this is really fear working on them. To get rid of the thinking and the fear, attack it right at the beginning.

If you're afraid you won't be able to get your voice out, yell the damn line. Afraid of being quiet? Whisper the line—barely audibly. Make everyone lean forward to hear. Afraid of moving—make a bold move. Afraid of standing still—stop moving and stand there like a rock!

What you fear, you must attack, the moment you become aware of it. Don't try to sneak into it. After you attack, take a breath in and out. Then go somewhere else—anywhere else—so you're not stuck in the same place. Go to the opposite choice or to any other different choice. It doesn't matter if you're right or wrong or if it's smart or stupid. What matters is that it will rid you of your fear. You will be free, and you will empower yourself.

You can't act when you're feeling weak. You can't really do anything when you're feeling weak. You lose the power to act—to do.

I remember my first professional audition. It was for several roles in a summer repertory company, including Cabot in Eugene O'Neill's *Desire Under the Elms*. I was particularly scared that I could never be strong enough for this powerful character and I had had almost no time to prepare.

I was on stage. I had just finished reading a scene from Arthur Miller's *A View from the Bridge* in which I had been moving all over the stage, full of anger and tears at the end. I took a deep breath, holding the O'Neill script in my hand. Then I looked down for a moment. I could feel the fear rising in me—the fear that I would have nothing for this character. So, I attacked my fear by doing nothing for a long time. I stood there. Didn't say a line, didn't move. The quiet was incredibly intense. Finally, I said the first line. Line by line I challenged myself. I let in what was there—what I felt—nothing else. And that's what I said with the line. I didn't move at all.

The director told me later, "When you did Cabot, you just stood there and said it. No one else did that. It was very powerful watching you just standing there with the book. I knew you could play this character and a lot more." I got the position in the company specifically because of that role, the one I had been most afraid of at the audition.

The best way to deal with fear is to attack it!

Take Control of the Audition

This is a bold strategy, but sometimes it's an effective one, as Mariel Hemingway once discovered.

Mariel had an audition for the movie *Creator*, in which she hoped to play a tough young woman who must seduce a genius (played by Peter O'Toole). The director and producer hadn't wanted to audition Mariel for the part. They saw her as too soft. Her agent insisted that they see her. I told her, "There's no way they're going to cast you in this role unless you take control of the audition." In fact, I told her, she had to make the director and producer a little scared of her, so that they were no longer sure *who* Mariel Hemingway was or what she was going to do. If they saw the Mariel they thought they knew, they wouldn't hire her.

She asked me how she could do that. I said, "When you walk in, if the chair you're to sit in is here, say to yourself, I don't think I want to sit there, and drag the chair—without saying anything about it to them—across the room to another spot that puts you in a different relationship to whomever you're going to talk to. Then keep doing things with the reader and with them that say, this is my audition and I'll do what I want! Make them figure out what the hell you're doing. Because if they don't have to do that, then you're not going to get the part."

She got it.

Jon Bon Jovi had a similar problem in his very first audition for a small, serious film, *Moonlight and Valentino*. The director didn't want to audition Jon, convinced that audiences would never be able to see beyond Jon the international rock star to accept him in the role of a down-to-earth housepainter. But Jon finally got seen, and in the audition, he had the courage to *not act at all*. He simply explored the scenes of the script without a trace of performing. The director was startled by Jon's ease and simplicity; he saw a guy with a sweet, gentle nature who was just another working class stiff. The Jon I knew, and the one the director discovered, was, in fact, perfect for the part (which he got that day).

Kevin Kline once unwittingly provided me with an excellent case study in the relative effectiveness of different approaches to auditioning.

The film director Alan Pakula contacted Kevin after seeing him in *The Pirates of Penzance* on Broadway. He told Kevin he was going to be directing a film of William Styron's novel *Sophie's Choice* and was seriously considering Kevin for the part of Nathan. "It's a wonderful character," he said. "I don't want to talk about it too much." He said he was months away from making any casting decisions and urged Kevin to read the novel in the meantime: "Then we'll talk some more."

"I said I would read the book and call when I was done," Kevin remembers. "I am the world's slowest reader. I am reading, and the more I read the more I realize that this character is a sort of genius! He knows everything about medicine, math, history, literature, art, music. I'm thinking, the longer I take reading this book, the dumber Alan will know I am, and the less chance I have of getting the part. But I can't speed-read. I'm thinking, I've got to lie and say I read it and loved it, get a synopsis of it and talk to someone about it. Luckily, while I was reading and worrying, Alan was busy doing another movie and I guess he never had the time to think that I was illiterate."

Pakula had told Kevin he wouldn't have to audition for him. But as Kevin and I talked about the situation, it became apparent to me that he *should* audition for Pakula. Months had passed and he still didn't have the part. No one had even called his agent. Kevin had yet to act in a film at that point. And many big-name actors with far greater reputations than his wanted a crack at what was, after all, a juicy role in an important film. As much as Pakula obviously liked him, Kevin was going to have to make it impossible for Pakula not to cast him.

So Kevin insisted on auditioning, or as he recalls it, "Harold insisted that I insist." He and I started preparing for the audition, which turned into two days of battling back and forth about what to do. Kevin said he "wanted to be off book and be able to blow the roof off." This is how most actors think they must approach auditions. I wanted him to do the opposite. I wanted him to explore the role in front of Pakula—just let himself improvise with the lines, taking it off the page piece by piece.

My reasoning was not theoretical. Kevin was used to working on stage, exploring the role in depth in rehearsal for weeks before performance. To try to "act" the role all of a sudden in front of the director at the very beginning of his work would make him feel rushed. The pressure of so little time would take away his legs. He would be thinking about results—something he would never do on stage. It would not be Kevin at all that Alan Pakula would see in that audition.

"We talked about the traps if you are playing someone that is a genius," Kevin remembers. "I wanted to do it 'right,' so I wanted to play someone who has glasses and wears a tie. I wanted to make a series of cliché choices that would say, I am the genius."

I believed the genius was in the script and Kevin just had to get out of the way. What I saw when Kevin took the lines off the page was that Nathan didn't have to look like an Einstein, bristling with a genius's eccentricities. Nathan was a schizophrenic who could be whoever he wanted to be at any moment. Kevin's instinct flew in all directions, taking him to magnificently strange choices. His natural responses moved incredibly fast, flying off a phrase to a place so unexpected and yet so real, personal, and brilliant that these sudden shifts in behavior seemed perfectly normal. But they didn't come together logically. And that was the character.

Any attempt to order this bizarre behavior would have been too obvious, not attractive and interesting enough for the film. You can analyze the pants off the character but you'll never find the territory that way. It's got to be impulsive. It has to happen in some sort of subliminal way or the audience will catch up with it too quickly.

I told Kevin that if Pakula saw him at work on the script as I had seen him—free, inventive, absurd, and intelligent—he would know Kevin was the only actor he could cast. Kevin was never more "Nathan" than when he was doing whatever he wanted to do at the moment. But this required Kevin to trust himself and his instinct completely.

After two days of working with me, Kevin went to audition. I made him promise he would start by taking it off the page.

He called me the next day, from the lobby of the Paramount building in New York. He had left the audition and called his agent, who had just gotten off the phone with Alan Pakula, calling to say, "Tell Kevin the part is his."

What happened at the audition?

Kevin did sit and take it off the page at first. He told me Pakula was really pleased with what he did. Then Kevin asked if he could do it again. Of course Pakula was interested in seeing more. So Kevin did the scene again. This time he was really going for it—moving, doing it from memory—"blowing the roof off."

When he finished the scene, there was a pause. After a couple of seconds Pakula said, "I like the first way better." Then he asked Kevin to stay and read the rest of his part in the script out loud with the casting director. He wanted to hear the role with Kevin's responses. So Kevin took the rest of the script off the page and landed the role.

It was too early for Kevin to perform at that audition. When performing, we are telling the director, This is it—this is what it should be. But we certainly don't know that at the beginning. And we may not even know that at the end. If we place our trust in our exploration of the text, then we are revealing to the director who we are in relation to this material. If we are performing, we are revealing only our "idea" about the character. The director may not see the actor through the acting.

What Kevin did when he took it off the page and explored the script was basically what he did in the movie. He was all instinct—like Nathan. He explored the scene in front of Pakula without caring where he went with it—without Acting. The lines took him to disconnected places that were all true to Kevin in the moment. Pakula could see that he could just film Kevin, and with Kevin's many different brilliant explorations, he could piece together an extraordinary character—brilliant, schizophrenic, scary, funny, charming, tender, delicate, masculine, and always unpredictable. He understood that the audience had to love him the way Sophie loved him in order for the film to make sense.

Of course, no matter how good you are in an audition, you still may not get the role. Remember, a good director won't cast you if he doesn't need *you*, even if he thinks you're a terrific actor. The director has a vision of the work, and his needs must be fulfilled with the right choice for him. It has nothing to do with us as actors. Sometimes we can surprise a director, by revealing sides of ourselves he didn't know we had, or by exciting him with a vision of the character he didn't think was possible. But all we can do is our best, and we must leave it to those casting to do their best.

And if we are consistently doing our best, we will be ready when the right part comes along.

Andie MacDowell came to me when no one would hire her. For a year and a half she came in week after week, working on her acting and preparing auditions. After a few months, she was really cooking. Her auditions started to show how talented she was, and the people she was auditioning for were impressed. But still no one cast her, and she was afraid she would never act again.

I told her, "Be patient. The right part is going to come along. And they'll have to have *you*." Then *sex, lies, and videotape* came along, with a hot new director, Steven Soderbergh. She auditioned, and Soderbergh absolutely had to have her in his film. He got his way. And she got the part. She was ready.

Be ready!

Suggestions for Practice

In addition to the scenes listed in chapter 1, here are some for audition practice.

Man / Woman	Noel Coward, *Private Lives*
	Sibyl and Elyot in Act I
Man / Woman	Neil Simon, *Barefoot in the Park*
	Paul and Corie in Act I
	Start "Corie? . . . Where are you?"
Man / Man	David Mamet, *Speed the Plow*
	Gould and Fox in Act I
	Start " . . . How much money could we stand to make?"
	End "but it ain't crowded".
Woman / Woman	Arthur Miller, *A View from the Bridge*
	Beatrice and Catherine in Act 1
	Start "Listen Catherine. What are you going to do with yourself?"
	End "Okay."
Man / Woman	Sam Shepard, *A Lie of the Mind*
	Frankie and Beth in scene 1
Man / Woman	Clifford Odets, *Golden Boy*
	Lorna and Joe in Act I, scene 4

Man / Woman	Tennessee Williams, *Summer and Smoke* Alma and John in scene 4 Start " . . . I want to see your father." Continue through the end of scene. Cut Dr. Buchanan and Rosa from the scene.
Man / Man	David Mamet, *American Buffalo* Don and Bob in Act II Start at the top of the scene. End "Teach and me and Fletcher."

The following are scenes from films.

Man / Woman	*Some Like It Hot* Joe and Sugar in scene 3
Man / Woman	*East of Eden* Abra and Cal in scene 1
Man / Woman	*Funny Lady* Billy and Fanny in scene 1 Start "I'm glad to see you Fanny." End "Gotta use your John, Kid . . . "

4

"Harold taught me that during rehearsal you must allow yourself to make an absolute fool of yourself if necessary. You cannot judge yourself. You must leave your taste behind."

—Kevin Kline

IN REHEARSAL

Theater has a built-in process that allows the actor to uncover the character: rehearsal. There are usually four to five weeks of rehearsal before the actor has to face an audience. In that time, the whole play will be staged with sets, lighting, costumes, music, sound, and any special effects needed. But most of all, rehearsal allows the actor to explore the possibilities of the character on his feet with the other actors and a director.

"The luxury of rehearsal to me is finding every way in which not to do it," Kevin Kline told me in our discussion about rehearsing. He continued, "To leave no door unopened. Not to deny yourself what may seem like inappropriate impulses."

In theater, rehearsal is the place to take chances, to make all of our mistakes. This is often a dilemma for the actor, who may be afraid of seeming inadequate to the director, the producer, and the other actors. He may even be afraid of being fired. But the more careful we are in rehearsal, the less range our characters will have in performance. If the actor hasn't explored the character enough in rehearsal to trust himself fully in performance, he will be dull when it's time to perform in front of an audience. And that's a real problem.

An actor must explore the character piece by piece, moment by moment, in rehearsal. He discovers what doesn't work or doesn't belong, not to fix the part in stone, but to leave himself free to continue the exploration in performance. By then, if the actor has gotten his big mistakes behind him in rehearsal, it will be a more informed exploration.

Here's a framework for thinking about the rehearsal period. First, when we are working at home, we are exploring on our own from our instinct, imagination, and also from our research. In rehearsal, we have other actors offering stimulation that affects us. In our homework we must be totally available to ourselves, and in rehearsal totally available to the other actors. But the real trick is to be available to ourselves while in rehearsal. We can't be pushed around by our response to the other actors or to the director, because we may lose ourselves. And only we are responsible, in the end, for our work.

The director's job is to put the play together during rehearsal in a cohesive way that moves the story along with the greatest clarity and speed. The actor's job is to make each moment of the character in the play believable, interesting, and thrilling. I think of our work, the actor's, as *exploding* the moment. The director's work is to *move it along*. You can see the potential for conflict here. But it is a necessary conflict if the play is to be fulfilled for the playwright and the audience.

Be Bold

When Kevin Kline was offered a part in the Broadway musical *On the Twentieth Century* in 1978, he called me to ask whether he should accept it. The role was the leading lady's handsome lover— a bit player in Hollywood movies of the 1930s. The script barely spelled out his character, so Kevin didn't have much to go on. But Harold Prince was directing, the book and lyrics were by Comden and Green, the music was by Cy Coleman, and Madeleine Kahn was starring.

"What's the problem?" I asked. "You have another job?"

"No," he said. "But the part is boring."

"Does it have to be?"

There was a pause on the other end.

"Right!" Kevin said finally. He decided to do it.

But while Kevin was waiting for rehearsals to begin, all he kept thinking about was how one-dimensional the part seemed to him. He feared he'd been hired only because he looked right for the part, nothing more. He thought the character had been written not as a comic part, but as the straight man. Every choice that occurred to him seemed as boring as the part did. At a loss and desperate to find the character, he impulsively filled his pockets with anything that came to mind as something a desperate, self-absorbed actor might use to draw attention to himself. He took every actor's fear—that he will make obvious, idiotic choices—to a lunatic extreme, selecting actual objects that were stupid, obvious, and idiotic. He was still worried, but at least he had acted on impulse.

Kevin's entrance was onto a train platform, in tow of the leading lady, whose appearance photographers were eagerly awaiting. At the very first rehearsal, Kevin grabbed a camera from one of the photographers, turned it on himself, reached into his pocket, and threw confetti into the air while he snapped a picture of himself. When he came into what was supposed to be a stateroom on the train in another scene, he reached into his jacket pocket, pulled out an eight-by-ten head shot of himself, and taped it to the rehearsal room wall. He thought Hal Prince would either like it or fire him. In fact, pictures of Kevin mysteriously popped up everywhere in rehearsals. He worried that all this would be perceived as desperate overacting and a ridiculous attempt at scene-stealing. But Hal Prince thought it was perfect for the character. He told Kevin to go as far as possible, and to trust him as director to rein Kevin in if necessary. Kevin's willingness to make a fool out of himself was the genesis of a vain, embarrassingly desperate and ambitious character—the quintessential "bit player." As a result, the part was built up over the rehearsal period, and a big song was added for Kevin's character. Eventually this "boring" role won Kevin his first Tony.

When I went backstage after an early preview to congratulate Kevin, he said, "But is it acting?"

"If it's not, who gives a damn?" I said. Then I explained why it was not just acting but good acting—unpredictable, startling, and refreshing.

When Kevin came to study with me he was a musician, a wonderful pianist, very sensitive, deep, cultivated—and tasteful. Unfortunately, I think good taste is antithetical to good acting because it stifles parts of the actor. Once he attacks his sense of good taste so that all the "cheap stuff" is out in the open—once he is in an uncensored exploration of the character—his taste becomes usable; it tells him what belongs and what doesn't. Having learned in his work with me to trust himself completely, Kevin had been freed from the shackles of good taste. As a result, he'd been able to tap into a part of himself that all actors have inside— the desperate need to be recognized.

In rehearsal, the actor has to shatter any preconceived notion he may have about the character—defy it, until he knows what the character is *not* by trying out precisely those possibilities that seem ridiculous. The actor must not play it safe in rehearsal. If he is to be ready by performance, he must make his mistakes as early as possible, because it can take a while to arrive at what the part is. Kevin remembers that it wasn't until he'd been clowning around for a while at a tech rehearsal of Sandra Jenning's *Beware the Jub-Jub Bird* that I directed off Broadway in 1976 that I insisted, "You must put that on stage, that's where you live as an actor."

This willingness to let go in rehearsal is not only essential to exploring comic characters. *It is necessary to work this way with a serious or tragic part as well.* The actor must be able to get beyond his shyness, good taste, and embarrassment from the very beginning of his work in rehearsal, like Aidan Quinn in *Streetcar* pulling the "meat" out of his pants. That doesn't mean the actor can't be simple or quiet or even delicate if that's where the lines and character take him. In rehearsal, the actor must give up Acting right from the beginning. He must have the courage to be simple, just to say the lines as he feels them, with no extras added—no beautiful projected speech, no graceful movement, no dramatics to fill out the character.

Take It Slow

In the best of all possible worlds, the rehearsal process starts out slow. In the first week, the actors and director sit around a big table, reading through the play. Performance issues are set aside so the actors and director can explore the play together. When a question comes up about a line, a scene, or the play as a whole, a discussion erupts. So everyone is working on the *same* play. Everyone takes their time and allows themselves to listen to the other actors explore their lines, creating a free communication back and forth.

Gradually, needing a physical expansion of their explorations with the other actors, actors start to get up from the table and move around in the scenes as they say their lines. The director sketches out the setting—the sink, the couch, the table, the doors through which the character's enter or exit on stage and where they lead.

The actors' free wandering converts to a need for direction. The director may have a specific blocking plan, but ideally he keeps it hidden at first, allowing the actors to find things—movement, props, etc.—on their own organically. Then, if their natural relationship to the character and scene works for the director, much of his work is done. If not, he can offer his pre-planned blocking and the actors will explore the new blocking.

The surprising thing is that if we start slowly at the beginning, everything becomes more natural and easy for both actor and director. Scenes start to play quicker and quicker. Because everyone is in it together, in no time actors are "off book," exploring more and more deeply with each other so that four or five weeks of rehearsal genuinely prepares them to explore in front of an audience.

But unfortunately, it doesn't always happen this way. Too often, within the first few days a director is already looking for results. And an actor becomes too intimidated to take his time. The director uses the rehearsal to stage and re-stage the scenes because it's never right the first, second, or third time when staging quickly without the actors' input—because it's not organic. And everything goes too fast. The director wants to see the performance and he wants it at performance tempo.

If everything is going too fast in rehearsal, the actor has to *work on his own, slowing everything down.* At night, take your lines slowly off the page. Don't worry about memorization—as we have discussed, it will happen naturally. Breathe, think, feel—let your instinct and imagination surface. Even if you are pressured to go faster than you want in rehearsal, you will not feel as rushed if you have been able to find space for yourself with the play on your own.

Do Your Homework

As I have said, I am not opposed to research as a tool for exploring character. In fact, used judiciously, it can be crucial to the rehearsal period, not only for the individual actor but for the production as a whole, as an early experience of mine illustrates.

I was cast in a play called *Second Avenue Rag* by Allan Knee at the Phoenix Theater in New York. It was about the garment trade in New York City in the early part of the twentieth century. I was to play a women's tailor in a dress shop that catered to stars of the Yiddish theater.

The first thing I did after being cast was to try to find out more about the period, the trade, and the Yiddish theater. I read books describing the history, art, theater, and politics of the era, and I found an old tailor in upstate New York, Willie Greenfield, who had emigrated many years ago from Germany. He was in retirement, but he took in odd jobs to keep busy. I became one of them.

Willie was a perfectionist. Each stroke—pierce, push, pull—was done perfectly and powerfully. He was never tentative in sewing. He was sweet but no pushover. There was a quiet strength about him. He was quite religious, in a very natural way. He had a deformity in his back that made walking difficult and painful, yet he never complained. He had great pride. He dressed simply but with style. He was thoughtful, but every now and then anger would burst from him. He seemed to love showing me how to work—he thought of me as an artist, so he showed me great respect even though I was much younger than him. He took his work seriously. He knew he was good. He didn't have to show off. Willie showed me that such men as the one I was to play not only existed but were interesting and full of life.

Willie had trained in Europe, and he showed me the difference between women's tailoring and men's tailoring—and the difference between the way men and women work at tailoring. First of all, they use different thimbles. The men use an open thimble, pushing the needle with the side of their middle finger. Women use a thimble that is closed on top and push the needle with the tip of the middle finger. I watched Willie closely—he had real force in his sewing. It was powerful and fast.

Willie gave me one of his old thimbles. I practiced all the time. When I went to rehearsal, I brought my sewing with me. Before long, I looked right and felt right. The sewing itself was a mess, but no one in the audience was going to see that. It made me laugh when I looked at it and became a part of the character— someone amused by his own work rather than bored.

I continued to sew as I read with the other actors, and as I was watching and listening to rehearsals from the side of the rehearsal room. When I was in a scene, Cynthia Harris, the actress playing the great Yiddish actress Bertha Kalish, would come over to check my sewing to see if it had gotten better, and we'd share a laugh. When I showed Willie's technique to the other two actors playing tailors, it changed the whole look of our work. Pretty soon, they started bringing their sewing to rehearsal too, and we sat together, watching and stitching and gossiping about our research, like a strange little kaffeeklatsch. Sewing quickly and powerfully, and listening to the bickering and bantering around me, I became a sort of spiritual leader to the tailors, with my skullcap, quiet manner, and amused disposition, which is how the character struck me.

When an actor's preparation is good, it impacts everyone in the production. It makes the actor fall in love with the character and everyone picks up on it. It makes them want to do more and it gives the work a dignity like that of Willie Greenfield.

Give Up Your Ego

I don't believe in talking in rehearsal about how I approach acting. For me, that is completely personal. I don't want anyone to know how I work, how I think. It's my secret—or, at least, it was. But I'm open to suggestion about everything as long as I'm free to do what I want. And since I never ask for permission, I always do what I want.

But I do let everyone else feel that I need their *help* to do my best work. And I do! If the other actors and the director believe that, they'll be of help. When something goes well, I give credit to them, even if they seemed to be a hindrance. After all, it may have been something they did that helped, even if I didn't realize it. Theater is a joint effort.

Here's an example of how you can use even another actor's apparent hindrance.

I was playing the character Biedermann in Max Frisch's play *The Firebugs* off-off Broadway in New York. He's a kind of everyman, as the name implies in German. But he is also a bully, if he thinks he can get away with it. The young actress playing Anna, a maidservant, was having trouble keeping up with me. She was trying to make too much of her lines, and the production was a mess.

So, I kept stepping on her lines. It was cruel but she was driving me crazy and I just couldn't wait for her. I really became a bully until she came to me one day, crying. She pleaded with me to let her get her lines out. I told her, of course I would, but what she had been doing was great for her and for me. It allowed me to be fierce on stage with her without Acting. And she was totally vulnerable to me and emotional in a way that was perfect for her character.

In rehearsal, give up your ego. Save it for your own personal awareness of who you are and how much faith you must have in your own talent and character to do well in this work. It will allow you to persevere when all looks bleak. But on stage in rehearsal, never take anything—that is, what is happening in the acting— personally. Make the assumption that everyone is trying to do his best. No one is trying to hurt you. It can be a very tense time. If you don't take things personally, you'll be better for it. *For me, everything that happens on stage is acting.* My feelings are real. What I see is what I see, and what I say with the line is what I mean. But when we are no longer acting the scene in rehearsal, I drop everything. Or, at least, I try.

Working with Direction

Great direction frees an actor to discover the character; it does not impose an interpretation of the character on him. Directors don't have to say much. They give us the room to explore, to fall on our faces, and then they help us up. And when we need a suggestion they offer it in a few words.

When Glenn Close starred opposite Jeremy Irons in *The Real Thing* on Broadway, Mike Nichols offered two memorable comments. "He told Jeremy that if we ever felt we were getting lost, to 'drown in each other's eyes,' " Glenn recalls. "And he said, 'Bring your day onto the stage.' "

Glenn was playing Annie—"a very hard part," a woman whom the audience perceives as extremely selfish. Instead of words, she has passion, "an inherent sexuality and freedom" that is terrifying to Henry, Jeremy Irons's character. Glenn knew she needed "to find the *feeling* in there, so it was free and fun. Otherwise it would be sort of deadly." Nichols's first direction allowed her to be totally sexual and passionate without having to do much—without having to Act. Just drowning in Jeremy Irons's eyes and having him return it was enough.

The second direction—"Bring your day onto the stage"—grounded Glenn, allowing her to be totally simple, as in her everyday life. "I'd stand in the wings with my grocery bag and say, Okay, I've just gotten out of my car. I've locked it. I'm walking up the sidewalk, and I've come in the door. I've come from a place that's very immediate and specific. And then it was, let's see what's going to happen!"

Everything is fair game in rehearsal. But it is not *just* for fun. It is necessary. Because we don't know where the character is going to emerge. We only know that it is going to emerge from us, from the alchemy of the script, our instinct, and sometimes, if we are lucky, with the help of the director.

Good directors like actors to surprise them. Come to a good director with the moxie to do whatever comes to you, and he'll help you to perfect your character. But sometimes we aren't so lucky with directors. Theater directors can be impatient. They may move too quickly to stage the play, blocking the actors' movements at the beginning of the rehearsal period and thereby forcing choices on them before any exploration of text and character has taken place. Or they may ask actors to memorize their lines and get "off book" too early, and then insist that they pick up their cues and their delivery speed, going for performance results long before that is possible. This kind of directing doesn't lead to ensemble acting. It leads to controlled, impersonal, technical acting. It gives all the actors the same rushed tempo and rhythm and takes away their chance to find the individuality of each character. Worst of all, in my opinion, it takes away the joy of exploring in rehearsal, which is my favorite part of acting. When Glenn Close talks of the joy of a "great direction" from Mike Nichols, she is responding to what is best about theater—the freedom to explore good writing openly with cast members and the director.

Each actor has to find a personal strategy for dealing with bad directing. In general, I advise actors not to get aggressive or angry. All that leads to is conflict. If you put a director against the wall, he'll bite you! But if you give him room, then anything is possible.

I believe in giving up our ego, not our work. So I don't argue in rehearsals. I listen. I move where I'm sent, and I always agree. But agreeing to a direction today doesn't mean I am going to do it tomorrow. I let the direction waft over me. If it makes sense or strikes a chord in me, I let it. But I don't try to remember it. If it's good, it will take hold automatically. If it's no good, it won't affect me. Either way, tomorrow I do whatever I do. If it's different from what the director wanted and he or the stage manager points it out, I apologize for forgetting. I take it on myself. I start to do what the director wants, and if it's uncomfortable or feels wrong, I admit it's my problem, whether it is or not. But I want the director to realize I'm *having* a problem. I'm not trying to *be* a problem.

This usually works because it's the truth. There's no ego involved, and therefore no argument. There is discussion, which is good. And the discussion itself has slowed down the process, which is what we need in rehearsal—the time to explore.

Sometimes, however, this approach is rejected by the director. "I don't know what to do," he'll say. "I'm trying to help you, but you won't take any of my direction."

In this situation, every actor must decide for himself what is at stake and how far he must go to achieve his ends. One actor, determined to avoid a protracted tug-of-war with a director, delivered an ultimatum: "You better fire me. If you find discussion and exploration threatening, we shouldn't work together." In this case, the director backed off, leaving the actor "to go freely down the road of exploration and have it be rich, because it came organically for me." In the end, he got to a place that was not unsatisfying to the director. But, he emphasizes, "If I hadn't been able to start my work that way in rehearsal, my performance would have been like a voice straining."

It is very important that the actor decide for himself how to work with a director who seems to be cutting off his ability to explore in rehearsal. The actor, and no one else, must take responsibility for his decision, because working this way can sometimes have a tough outcome. On the other hand, allowing his instinct to be stifled will lead to a failure that may be worse for the actor than being fired—a haunting disappointment that he was unable to do his best work. When you are in this situation—between a rock and a hard place—don't blame yourself or anyone else. If you decide to continue, keep your focus on the play, and on the joy of exploration.

The only way to work through all this is to trust yourself. If you just go where you think the director wants you to go, you will have to fake it, and that will only weaken you as an actor. Continue to explore and you will eventually have the best crack at solving any problems that you and the director are facing. Don't blame yourself and don't lose heart; problems are the reason for rehearsals. Most of all, don't succumb to fear.

Exploring and Repeating

So if rehearsal is a constant process of exploration, how and when is it possible for an actor to authentically repeat choices he has discovered? If the choice came out of an exploration that was potent for the actor—if it has genuine meaning and power for him—repeating is usually no problem, because he wants to go there again. He feels free every time he makes that choice.

For example, at the opening of the second act of *Second Avenue Rag*, the tailors were supposed to be on an excursion on the Hudson River to celebrate the Fourth of July. The first time we rehearsed on our feet, I entered, came to the front mark on the floor, and looked out at what I thought would be New York Bay. I saw the director, the stage manager, and some actors sitting next to the rehearsal room wall. I looked at them and past them, smiling. It's nice, I thought, out on the water, with a cool breeze, the smell of the river. I let my gaze flow to the right. I stopped, squinted through my glasses. Everyone was quiet, watching me. I concentrated on what I was seeing in my imagination. My right arm started to move over my head as my left hand came to my chest. My right hand was clasped around a torch and my left held a book, and I started to grin at the joy of discovering the Statue of Liberty right there in the rehearsal room. Everyone laughed. The other two tailors entered, and they too looked to the statue.

I hadn't thought of doing that before the rehearsal. I thought I'd look out at the sunny sky and take a big breath of fresh air, feeling chipper and young away from the sweat shop. But as I looked around the room, I rejected that choice as too routine, and my imagination pictured the statue, in a bit of mist at first. I thought maybe it was my bad eyesight, or a trick. Then it became so clear to me that I just had to physicalize the image. It was silly but it's what I felt at the moment, and it worked perfectly for the character and the play.

Each time that scene came in rehearsal, I went on stage and let it happen—and most of the time it did. But one day I thought there must be something better, so I didn't do the statue. I don't know what I did, but it was as dead as a doornail. I asked the director, Gerald Freedman, what he thought.

He was a very experienced and helpful director. He said, "Harold, sometimes you hit it just right early in rehearsal and you have to admit you've got it. Leave it alone." And so I did, and it was always a special moment. But I had needed to go beyond that choice in order to return to it freely.

In rehearsal, we may discover a choice that works well. The actor is happy. The director is happy. But this still may not be the *best* choice. The only way for the actor to know is to keep on exploring. If in the process nothing works as well as the earlier choice, then the actor knows it is right. Even better, he *feels* it is right. Then repeating the choice is no problem.

IN PERFORMANCE

Although being on stage in front of an audience seems like a frightening place to be, as in auditioning, the worst thing the actor can do is try to protect himself or look for safety. It's not that he won't be afraid. He will be. But when he attacks his fear, he also attacks his intellect, which leaves him with only his instinct to rely on. If an actor is meant to be an actor, he will work best when he is out there on the edge.

Enter with Maximum Freedom

It's important not to make too many specific choices for the character in advance. If we do, we will leave ourselves no room to really respond on stage. In performance, too many predetermined choices don't make us feel secure; instead, we worry about executing all those choices. Deciding just a few points gives us beacons. The rest will be open to improvisation and exploration.

At the first preview of Kevin Kline's first *Hamlet* at the New York Shakespeare Festival, he found his performance deadened by the number of advance decisions he'd made. Whatever the reasons for those choices—perhaps the director's need to control the production, or perhaps the fear every actor experiences when approaching this massive, daunting role—every moment now felt heavy to him. It wasn't Kevin's Hamlet yet.

Night after night in front of the audience, Kevin stripped away the choices he'd made in favor of explorations that were alive in the moment. After a few weeks, he was left with only those points that were truly necessary and important to the illumination of the character: his first entrance, dark and relentlessly unforgiving of his mother; certain moments toying with a fierce playfulness with Claudius, Polonius, and Rosencrantz and Guildenstern; his lewd, vulgar, raging scene with Ophelia; and his speech to the Players, during which he put on clown-face.

As for the rest, he allowed the script to take him wherever it went each night. These explorations were informed by the work Kevin had done in rehearsal, on his own, and now in performance. The difference was extraordinary. It was not a meandering, unclear performance but exactly the opposite. It was clear at every moment, with a momentum that built inevitably to its conclusion. It was filled with a mercurial life and surprise. This Hamlet was thoughtful, witty, cruel, outrageous, raging, and loving—unpredictable, yet totally comprehensible. *This* was Kevin's Hamlet.

Repeating and Exploring—Reprise

In performance as in rehearsal, the actor is free to repeat a choice—and if he has thoroughly explored the character in rehearsal, he will most often find himself repeating some of the potent choices he has discovered. But he always has to give himself the option of *not* repeating a choice—of going somewhere else at that moment. If he doesn't, his acting will be dull, no matter how good the choice is. He will know what is coming, and he will unconsciously telegraph this to the audience. He will get ahead of himself on stage, because he will be thinking about what's coming, not where he is at that moment. His instinct will shut down. He may think he is safe, but his acting will have lost its edge.

You need a sense of freedom to be creative and alive on stage, up to and including performance. You need to feel that you can do anything you want, at any moment, or your acting will lack spark, and the character will be flat. If you feel obligated to do what you're going to do, there will be no surprise for you, and therefore no surprise for the audience. You have to carry the freedom of rehearsal into performance.

If you truly believe in a choice you have discovered earlier in rehearsal, or in a previous performance, and it matters to you greatly, you must trust yourself completely and forget about the specific choice until it comes up. You must absorb yourself in each moment prior to the choice, so fully that you can't think of the choice ahead. You must be open to each moment, including the possibility that you will make a choice other than the one you made in rehearsal. I may think, maybe I won't do the Statue of Liberty tonight. Then, when I come out on stage, perhaps I see a seagull and lose myself in it. And when it flies off, I may look around sadly and see . . .

The greater the distance between where you are and the choice that is coming, the more surprising it will be for both you and the audience when it does come—as long as you stick to the text! When the moment does come, you are free to make the choice in the same way you did last night or, for that matter, the last forty nights, as long as you make the decision at that very moment. Then whatever choice you make will be fresh.

When Choices Stop Working

Often in performance everything goes well for us. We are feeling free because we are trusting ourselves and exploring the text, freely repeating choices that continue to have meaning for us. But when what we are doing isn't working in performance, we must be bold in exploring other choices, as bold as at the outset of rehearsal.

A number of years ago, I was acting in a play by Romulus Linney called *Tennessee*. Frances Sternhagen, an important and wonderful actress, played the leading role, and I played Griswold Plankman, the suitor who not only tricks her into marriage but makes her believe that she is traveling with him over the mountains and through the forests all the way to Tennessee, never to see her family again. In the end, after they have lived together for many years and Griswold has died, she is wandering the hills, lost, when she comes upon her parents' house. She realizes that all the time she and Griswold had been living only a few miles from her parents' home. But without Griswold's trick, she would never have had a full life. Her intransigence and difficult personality would have left her an old maid. It was a countrified *Taming of the Shrew*.

During rehearsal, Frannie and I had a great time playing off each other. The writing was very good, and we just let the dialogue take us. Griswold Plankman was a jokester. He spoke in puns and made me feel like fooling around a lot. So I kept trying different choices in rehearsal, never settling on anything. Frannie was generous in her acting and open to everything. I had great respect for her talent, experience, and intelligence, and she was a joy to act with. What could be better?

When we went into technical and dress rehearsals and began previews, however, a curious thing happened to me. I found myself too aware of the staging, of where I thought I was expected to be for Frannie at any given moment. Before going on stage, I found myself running my lines over and over—something I never did. I was tense while waiting for my entrance, and the entrance started to feel unnatural. On stage I felt uncomfortable. I became conscious of picking up my cues and getting laughs. I felt locked in. My acting became flat. It was as if I had no space around my lines. Worst of all, I felt dull!

There was no joy for me in the performance. This had never happened to me before on stage or in film. I couldn't figure out what was going on.

At one performance, Kevin Kline and about twenty of my students were in the audience. I had always liked that sort of challenge. But the same thing happened. Afterward, Kevin and I talked. He didn't seem bothered. He recognized the problem of feeling flat. It was reassuring, he said, that it could happen to his teacher. But I was ready to shoot myself.

The next evening when I came to the theater, I didn't go over my lines. I spent the time before performance reading material for the next day's coaching, a novel—anything but the script. When I got the call for places, I walked to the stage. I had no idea what I was going to do. I only knew what I wasn't going to do. I wasn't going to stay where I was.

I entered and looked around. I didn't walk to the spot I normally did. I went calmly to another part of the stage and delivered my line. The line came out with abandon, and it got a big laugh—which it was supposed to get.

Frannie came rushing over to me, delivering her line as she ran. She barely got to me when I casually strolled across the stage to the other side, saying my line. Another big laugh. Now that I didn't care where I went on stage, I was no longer worried about my lines. I felt free.

Frannie flew across to me. She was furious with me on stage. Even though this was right for her character and this wonderful story about an impossible relationship, I thought her anger might be personal, that she might feel I was messing up her performance. But I'll tell you this: we were really cooking. And although we were improvising each moment, we stuck to the lines. We found a freedom and reality between us that was both fresh and edgy. She was with me every step of the way.

When the lights went down, I exited just behind her in total darkness, as I always did. We were barely off stage when I felt hands on my face. I braced myself. I thought Frannie was going to belt me one.

Instead, she planted a big kiss on my lips. Then she hugged me and said, "Where have you been, Harold?"

What had happened? My fear had sneaked up on me in performance. Instead of attacking it, I looked for safety. I stopped exploring. I froze up, went flat. It was no longer me on that stage—no longer my Griswold for Frannie.

I stress the importance of continuing the exploration in performance not to subvert directors' work but precisely because the shared work of the actor and director is so important, and it has to be alive in the performance. No director wants a replica of what he's worked on. He wants the performance alive and full of the same kind of energy and stimulation that was in play when actor and director came up with their first successful choices in rehearsal. That's what live theater is about. Actors need directors. But directors also need actors at their best in performance.

Performance doesn't always require such drastic choices to keep us at our best. But sometimes we have to actively shatter our fears, our obligations, our preconceptions to free ourselves for our best work. We must put ourselves in danger, on the edge, to make instinct surface. If all we know is what we will say but not how we will say it, instinct will be free to take us there in a newly creative way. Once we are cooking again, many of the choices we had made before may recur. We may not need to keep changing things so boldly.

No specific choice is more important than the true presence of the actor on stage at that moment. The actor, alive on stage, with his humanity—his feelings, his thoughts, his imagination—intact, is the greatest gift he can give the audience.

So the actor must be patient. He must not preempt the thoughts and feelings that come to him on stage in the moment. If he gives himself time in that frightening moment, something may come to him that is better than what he had—maybe something surprising. And he must have the courage to go with whatever truly matters to him at the moment, whether it's something he already knows or something new. It may seem scary to do this in performance, but the actor owes the audience the best he's got, whether he has discovered it in rehearsal or that very night. The audience has given up their precious time. They have paid to see us. They trust we will give them our best. We must not only trust the work we've done in preparation. We must trust ourselves and our connection with the text to take us *in performance* to the best choice we have to offer.

For me, that is what acting on stage is all about.

Acting in Long Runs

Acting in a long run on Broadway, in regional theater, or on tour can bring many challenges. After a couple of months of eight performances a week, the actor can go on autopilot—beginning to think he knows where the laugh is, where the pauses are, where to move, how each line goes. This doesn't make for good acting or a thrilling experience for the audience. Boredom sets in, making each performance a chore.

Glenn Close recalls that when she and Jeremy Irons were about four months into *The Real Thing* they were so bored that one night after the first act they met in Jeremy's dressing room and he said, "Okay, let's go out in the second act and surprise each other. Let's go to different areas of the stage. Let's do anything to jerk ourselves out of this rut."

"By that time the set was like home," she remembers. They were so familiar with it, it was easy to try new things, and trying new things got the adrenaline pumping again and "jolted us out of the doldrums." They kept exploring and trying to surprise each other, and they kept some of the new choices they made. "We would always meet after the first act and say, 'That worked. Why don't we try that tomorrow?' Or, 'That didn't. Why?' That's the joy of having a great piece of material in the long run."

Kevin Kline called me one night after a performance of *Pirates of Penzance* on Broadway. He had been in the show for several months following two months at the Delacourt in Central Park. It was a huge hit and he had been nominated for a Tony Award. He wanted me to come back and see the show, particularly his performance.

"What's the problem, no laughs?" I asked.

"No, they're laughing," he said. "It's just that the audience doesn't have that immediate response they had in the park and when we first opened on Broadway. Tell me what you see. We're selling out and the Tony voters are returning for a second look."

I went the next night. Sure enough, Kevin was good—fun to watch, getting a lot of laughs—but he was ahead of himself. He knew where the laughs were. So he was there before the audience was, and then on to the next moment before the audience could truly respond to what he had just done so brilliantly.

I suggested that Kevin forget about the big laugh moments and concentrate only on the moment he was in on stage—even if it meant changing how he played each moment. He could make little changes or big ones as long as they forced his concentration onto that moment alone. When the big laugh moments came up they would be fresh. But he must not rush them. "The audience needs to be with you," I told him. "For instance, when Frederic tells you that he is leaving and he is indentured until noon this day, you look straight up at the sun and say, 'But it is not yet twelve o'clock?' Instead of just looking up and then saying the line, do a double-take or even a triple-take, and then say the line. After all, the Pirate King is dense. He may not be sure why he looked up. He may have forgotten it was to check the time." We talked through a number of such moments.

The next night Kevin called from his dressing room at intermission to tell me that he'd done six takes on the sun before he finally said the line. The audience was roaring, and they were with him all the way through the act. His performance was back on track because he was free to explore it anew.

Long runs give the actor the possibility of going into the role in greater depth—*if* the actor is willing to surprise himself and stay on the edge. The playing field only gets bigger and bigger, with greater opportunities and variations.

In acting, the trip is what's interesting, not the destination.

Acting is the trip!

5

ACTING IN FILM AND TELEVISION

"You taught me how to prime myself, like a gun—put together, cleaned, cocked, loaded, and ready to go. I did not know how to do that for myself. I didn't even know how to begin. I didn't even know the mechanism was supposed to be a gun . . . because you've got to be ready to fire."

—Bridget Fonda

Unlike theater, film and television usually have no prolonged rehearsal period. Instead, the whole filming period from which the actor's performance on screen will be drawn is one giant rehearsal.

On stage, the actor's performance on that night is the character in total. No editing is possible—it's all you. The actor in film does not have the opportunity to complete the character as he does on stage. In the end, the director will put the character together in the editing room.

Therefore, the director has the actors play each scene again and again in front of the camera. Each "take" is just another exploration. If what the actor has done seems good to the director, he calls, "Cut. Print." This means that piece of film will be sent to the laboratory to be developed so that the director and editor can see the scene in "dailies" as a possibility for editing into the final cut of the movie. If it's not good for the director, he calls, "Cut. Let's do it again." If the actor blows his lines or screws up an action, it doesn't really matter. It is best to continue the take. It's not necessary for the whole take to be perfect, because a whole take is rarely used in the final cut. If a piece of a take is good, that piece will be used.

There are rare exceptions. Woody Allen, for example, likes to use only a master-shot for each scene. He doesn't have "coverage," in which there are many shots at different angles and distances. In this kind of filming, the director will rehearse a great deal and take a long time to complete the master shot. It will take as long to shoot this one shot as it takes to shoot the many shots for a scene in traditional American filmmaking. The whole take has to be perfect, because there are no possibilities of editing within the scene. It's like acting in a play.

But most of the time, filming is, as Glenn Close describes it, "like one big rehearsal without the performance at the end of it." Knowing this can be extremely liberating for the actor. As Glenn says, "You can loosen up. You can breathe. You can try things. There's such a huge flexibility in film. That, to me, is what's fun about movies."

During the filming of *Sophie's Choice*, Alan Pakula told Kevin Kline, "Think of it as rehearsing, and trust the moment in the rehearsal. When it really happens, that's the take I'm going to use." If you think of film this way, then the process of creating a character for film becomes clear. The actor cannot control how the character will ultimately be perceived. But between "action" and "cut," it's all the actor. So you must be free in each take, and with each take you must be trying out different ways to play the scene. You must offer many possibilities "within the parameters of the character," as Glenn puts it, "so that the director will have a choice—a valid choice."

PREPARING THE ROLE BEFORE FILMING BEGINS

When Bridget Fonda is cast in a film, she comes to me to "pre-rehearse," as she calls it. "I work with you to rescue the rehearsal period," she says.

Directors want and expect a professional actor to bring a great deal to the table. He has to be available to the director, but as Jim Gandolfini says, "You should have your own idea. You should try to surprise the guy a little bit." Most directors hope that the actor will surprise them with ideas about the character. And if the actor has done the preparation to put himself into a state of open exploration with the character, he will be available to whatever the director has to offer. He will come to filming with possibilities to offer, and with a confidence in his work that gives him the strength to do his best.

"I kind of want to have my cake and eat it too," Bridget says, about opening herself to both her own exploration of the character and the director's insights. "It's, How can I satisfy the truth of this and yet be able to go anywhere with the director? If you're lucky enough to be with someone who is a genius, you want to get that gold they have to offer. And yet you can't compromise yourself, because it has to stay free. It can't be contrived. And that is the biggest trick." Instead of trying to anticipate what the director wants, the actor prepares by "completely investigating" the character, discovering as many possibilities as he can before filming begins without making any decisions. He can explore alone or with a coach. The steps are the same and easy to replicate on your own.

Take the Script off the Page

First, I take the actor through the script from beginning to end, having him verbalize his lines by taking them off the page. We read back and forth, letting the lines take us wherever they go. As Bridget says, "The lines are your lifeline." Then we go over the scene, pulling it apart, plumbing the nuances of each moment, making sure the actor is in tune with himself, the scene, and the lines. We do each scene many different ways. We take our time.

On your own, you must work out loud, verbalizing your lines, the other characters' lines, and even your thoughts, as I described in chapter 3. Don't skim—really immerse yourself in every line, letting your mind wander around what's happening with the character. Take each scene off the page in five different ways, as I suggested earlier—for example, in a rage, for laughs, for intimate internal values, for sensuality, for pure logic. Don't set anything; just try out ideas.

Work Through the Script in Sequence

It is even more important in film than in theater to work your way through the script in sequence, because films are shot out of sequence. Working in sequence helps you to discover the character by osmosis, not analysis. As you go from beginning to end, verbalizing not only the lines but your reactions to them, the character simply appears, as does the meaning of the story as a whole. "It's kind of like when you do a play," James Gandolfini says, "and you rehearse scenes three, four, and five, and six, seven, and eight, but you don't really know the character until you do a run-through of the whole thing. And then you go, Oh! And something happens— the guy starts to come to life and you get the whole thing."

As the actor and I read back and forth, coming to know each moment in a specific way, the actor becomes aware of the intimate changes that are happening within each scene to the character. Even if the actor has read the script to himself from start to finish, it doesn't really come to life until he begins to speak the lines out loud. As James Gandolfini says, "I'll know I can do a role, but it doesn't take shape sometimes until I talk it out."

Sometimes it's a particular line that brings the character into focus. "We kind of close the net," Bridget says. "It starts out in a general way and then gets down to the lines—to the crux of the moment. There's this one line that's going to be the key, that's going to say it all about the character. When that falls into your lap, you don't want to miss it—not know what it was. You don't want to choke on it. You want to be able to do something great with it. That's when we work on this line, this line, this line. It's so abstract and yet it's the whole idea of this story."

But whether it's a single line that brings the character to life or a number of moments in the story, the actor has to know the script cold, to feel it in his bones, so that he's free to be in an improvisational state when he's filming. If he's thinking about where he was in the previous scene, or where he's supposed to end up in the next scene, the camera will catch him Acting. *And the camera is unforgiving about Acting.* To be believed on film, you must be living in the moment, going with the impulse as it hits you.

In the end, the actor needs to work on the script in sequence so that it is so much a part of him he doesn't have to think about the story at all while filming. Then his only concern is what's playing on him at the moment of shooting. The script will move the story along anyway, but the moments will be filled creatively. This will make the story more surprising and the character less predictable to the audience, because they too will be lost in each moment and will have to put each moment together with the story as it develops. Remember, when the audience is involved and has to work, it becomes active and interested rather than passive and bored.

Research What You Don't Know

As with stage acting, research has its place. As I go through the script with an actor, we pinpoint aspects of the script that call for investigation. Working on your own, pay attention to what you don't know and do research on that.

For example, John Leguizamo and I were working recently on a new film, *Infamous*. He was to play Lex Vargas, a Puerto Rican boxer who becomes middleweight champion. John is a marvelous actor, but he wasn't a boxer, so he had to start training as a boxer. But as we worked our way through the script, we also spent a lot of time discussing how boxers think and what makes a champion.

I told John about an experience I had coaching the great fight trainer Teddy Atlas for a role in a boxing film. Teddy, an early trainer of Mike Tyson, also trained the heavyweight champion Michael Moorer. Teddy told me his idea about personal character as it relates to genuine champions in the ring. He talked about the "negatives," like bullies, and the "positives"—those who know themselves, won't allow loss, and are true champions. Just listening to and watching Teddy talk can tell an actor a lot about boxers—the tics, the rhythms, the permanent bruises.

I suggested John get in touch with Teddy as a source of information that would be invaluable for the character of Lex. We also talked about styles of boxing relating to ethnicity, which could affect his performance.

There are times when the research you do on a character will contradict aspects of the script. This doesn't invalidate the process.

In fact, everything an actor does finds its way into his work and has a subliminal impact that makes the character more interesting.

When Jennifer Connelly was preparing the role of Alicia Larde in the film *A Beautiful Mind*, she researched the character of Sylvia Nasar, on whom the role was based. Although she couldn't use many of the real-life details because the script differed from them, her research informed our discussions and gave the character a deeper layer that resonated with the audience.

I talk with actors about anything the script brings to mind from my own life and experience. You may want to talk to people who know something about your character or his circumstances, or find out what the story means to them. Listen to them and take what is useful. But don't ask them how you should play the character. That's your job. Be open without making any decisions.

Make Big, Extravagant Choices

Actors often think they can't make extravagant choices—be "big"—in film because it will look too extreme on screen. *But size doesn't matter. Truth does.* In film, the settings, even period settings, are real. If the actor makes a choice that has more to do with style than reality, no matter how conservative it is, it won't work. And conversely, if the moment is totally real for the actor and true for the character, the audience will buy it, however big or exotic.

Most of the time I am trying to get actors to do less on film—to let the camera do the work of acting while the actor allows himself simply to respond, listen, and talk without *showing* what he's feeling or thinking. But we must be free to go anywhere, including big, extravagant choices. Bigger is not necessarily better, but it *is* necessary not to censor your response, because those risky, bold choices are often our best. The actor's unbridled instinct, when totally truthful, can add an element of danger or absurdity that can make a good script an astonishing one or take an actor's career from good to great.

Kevin Kline's character in *A Fish Called Wanda* is a perfect example of how big and outrageous a character can be on film. Otto is stupid, dangerous, easily frustrated, and easily enraged by any reference to his stupidity. When he opens a safe and finds it empty, his confusion and rage lead him to shoot this inanimate object as if it were a person he wished to kill. His sexuality is based on smells and Italian food terms, and his idea of torture involves shoving French fries up a character's nostrils and eating his pet fish. It's all idiotic, but it's the character.

As I described in chapter 2, the genesis of this character emerged while Kevin and I were taking Otto's lines off the page. Before filming begins, go as far as possible if something strikes you. Once you're shooting, take your chances. If it's too much, the director will tell you. However, you must keep exploring and doing different things each "take." Be brave. Make a fool of yourself. Remember, filming is the same as rehearsal.

ON SET

Just before shooting begins, the actor and director meet to talk about the character and specifically how each sees him dressed— his costume. This is very important because then there are costume fittings, as well as make-up and hair tests for camera. So the actor must know the script and character in order to offer insight into the way the character should appear on camera.

Sometimes there are rehearsals for a few days or a week with the director and other actors, during which time rewriting, discussions about the script and locations, and even some blocking for specific scenes may take place. But as a whole, it's not the same as the long period of rehearsal in theater. It is best for the actor to stay loose during these rehearsals. Use the time to get a feeling for the other actors. Don't worry about any decisions made here. They will not matter once the director and cast are on location. Then, the acting and shooting will be stimulated by the reality of the set.

Many actors like rehearsals in film, but I don't. It isn't enough time to really rehearse but it's enough time to tighten the actor if he takes it too seriously. So stay loose! Explore as much as you can but don't give too much away at this point. This is usually not the best situation to show everything. Save it for the filming, when it's for real.

The same goes for the read-through of the script that will take place with the whole cast in front of the director, the writer, the producers, and the studio executives. This occurs just after camera tests and rehearsals. It's often a harrowing experience for the actors, but there's no reason to worry. No matter what is said here or in rehearsal, it is the actual shooting that counts.

The key thing is to keep the process of exploration going all the way through the shooting process. When Kevin Kline got ready to film *A Fish Called Wanda*, I told him that it was necessary to improvise in character with the cast and crew as he came onto the set for each scene. His character was so bold that he had to do this as a way of warming up for the takes. He told me he continued improvising between takes as well. Often an actor isn't finished with the possibilities of a take when the camera stops shooting. Continuing gives the actor and the director more choices, choices that can be incorporated into the next take.

Don't consciously try to repeat an impulse that worked. Actors often say something like, "This one take was great. The director loved it, but the lighting or the sound wasn't right. When we re-shot it, I couldn't get it back, and we did a lot of takes." If this happens, don't try to get it back. Go somewhere else, anywhere else. Even if you blow the next take, the take after that you will be back on your instinct and back into exploring.

Working with Direction

All the good directors I have known either say very little and let the actor work it out, or they make good suggestions that they are perfectly willing to let go in favor of the actor's instinct. Kevin Kline recalls that on the set of *Sophie's Choice*, Alan Pakula told him, "Whatever I said before the take, if you get an impulse, fuck what I said!" This is a very smart and generous thing for a director to say, because it empowers the actor. It gives him the freedom to be impulsive, and that is best for the film as well as for the actor. Unfortunately, it is rare for a director to make such a comment.

There are many distractions for the director during filming. He's responsible for every choice made—not just the actor, but also the costumer, the director of photography, the set designer, set decoration, props, sound, and on and on. So he has a lot to do. Because of these distractions, the acting is often the last thing on the director's mind. It's difficult, almost impossible, for him to stop everything in order to truly concentrate on a scene or fragment of the scene, and it's easy to miss subtle acting. Usually, everything seems too slow for the director. The most common direction on set is "pick up the pace," "get rid of the pauses," "speed up the rhythm."

It's important for the actor to remember that the scene as you do it is unedited. Eventually, the director can cut out pauses in the editing room. So take your time and respond instinctively and impulsively. That will be best not only for you, but in the end for the director as well. I'll explain more about this in the section on playing the close-up.

It takes a long time to set up a shot. The lighting and camera crew will be at it for a couple of hours or more before the actor is called to the set. Directors have producers and production supervisors pushing them to shoot fast. But the acting will probably be the shortest part of the filming process. So if you are not finished with the shot and think you can do better, even if the director is satisfied, ask for another take. Most directors will be pleased to give you another go at it because it may lead to something much better. And it really doesn't take much time. Once they go to the next shot, there is no chance for another crack at the moment.

Acting on the Day of Shooting

Let me give you an overview of the shooting day as it almost always happens. Shooting the scene is usually geared to the technical demands of camera, lighting, and set, not to the actor. The filming starts from a distance, taking in the whole scene in the master shot, and then gets closer and closer as the day goes on. So at first, everyone in the scene will be filmed from beginning to end. Then, as the camera gets closer, the shooting gets more specific. Usually, in the name of technical efficiency, the camera will film all the shots from one side, that is, getting closer and closer on one actor first. For instance, if there are two actors in the scene, the next shot will be a medium "two-shot"—that is, the actors will be shot from the waist up—followed by shots that (1) show the actors in profile, (2) favor one actor, and (3) capture the actor over the shoulder or back of the other actor. Finally, there will be a close-up shot on only one actor. Then, when that actor's close-up is completed, the camera is moved to the opposite angle and the crew re-lights and re-dresses the set for the same shots on the second actor. Usually, all the takes will be shot from beginning to end. If there are more than two actors in the scene, the process will be repeated for each actor. So the actor goes over the scene from beginning to end, again and again, both on-camera and off-camera, over the course of the day.

You must give the best you have on the day of shooting. On film, that's the only day for that scene. You have to trust yourself on that day. Because in the end, you know more about the character than anybody else in the room. If you don't, you're not good enough to play the character. It's as simple as that. The director may have a million things on his mind on the day of shooting, but an actor has only one.

The Master Shot

The filming day starts with the master shot, in which the actors run the scene from beginning to end. The shot is a large one that takes in the full scene. The actor doesn't have to define the way he will play the whole scene in this shot. It is a general outline of the blocking of the scene. In the final cut of the movie, the master will be used mostly to establish the setting. Little if any of the acting in it will be used in the final edit.

First, the actor is called to the set to rehearse the scene with the other actors, the director of photography, and the director. The scene does not yet have to be memorized. (The "sides" for the day—the scenes to be shot—are copied and distributed to the whole company first thing in the morning.) It's usually a relaxed rehearsal. After rehearsing, the actors are off to costume and make-up, while the lighting is adjusted for the camera and the set is dressed.

During this time (an hour or two), the actor can go over the scene and finish memorizing, if necessary, or he can look over the previous scene in his trailer. But there's no reason to get anxious. This is only the beginning of the day.

The actor will be recalled to the set and a few more rehearsals will take place to set the marks for the actor. A mark is a taped line on the floor placed by the camera crew for the actor. That mark indicates where the actor must stop a movement to be in focus within the scene. This often creates a lot of problems for young actors because if they are too aware of the mark and too diligent about hitting it, their movement may seem false or awkward. And if they are delivering lines as they move, those lines may sound stilted because of the distraction. But if you don't hit the mark, you're out of focus, so the scene is stopped.

It is best to look at the mark and walk over to it several times just to feel out the move in rehearsal. When "action" is called, forget about it. You either hit the mark or you don't, but worrying about it will screw up your acting. Remember, this is film. If you miss your mark you get to do it again. It's useless to hit your mark and not be free. Sometimes the crew will put a sandbag on the floor as a mark so you can't miss it. But don't think about it when shooting begins. (Supposedly, Spencer Tracy would walk up to his mark, look down to make sure he had hit it, and then say his line. No one ever bugged him about it.)

Don't give too much in the master shot unless the director tells you that this is the shot he is going to use in the final edit. Keep it simple. Don't worry about flubbing your lines. You've got plenty of takes to get it right.

The Camera Moves Closer

As the camera moves closer, the scene comes more and more into focus for the actor as well as for the audience. But there is still a long way to go until the close-up. Scenes can take several hours, even a whole day or more, to film. And the last shots are the most important. It is crucial that the actor stay emotionally loose through the process and not give all his emotions away until the close-up. Otherwise, he will be used up by the time he needs those emotions most.

So the actor has to pace himself. He must keep his concentration available for the take, but in between set-ups for each shot—gaps of about two hours, usually—he should not think about the scene or expend a lot of energy. In emotional scenes, young actors tend to over-prepare and to spend themselves before the most important shots of the day. It's a long day, typically ten to fourteen hours. If you have prepared yourself before the day of shooting, don't press now. Wait until just before the take to get back into it. Stay calm, and your concentration will be accessible when you need it.

The Close-Up

The close-up is what movies have that theater doesn't. With the close-up, as Glenn Close puts it, "You can look straight into somebody's soul."

The close-up can be the easiest shot for the actor, or the hardest. The closer the camera, the less the actor has to do. If he is in the moment, everything he is thinking or feeling, and every shift in what he thinks or feels, registers. But because the camera is such a sensitive instrument at close range, if the actor *shows* us what he's thinking or feeling, it will be too much. *He must not demonstrate his thoughts or feelings.*

This is where trust comes in. The actor must trust himself, and only himself, to know if he is feeling or thinking. He can't trust anyone else to take his measure at that moment. And that holds true even when the director asks him to give more. During the shoot, the director may be distracted, or he may be watching the actors on a television monitor, where subtle reactions are difficult to see and nothing looks like it's enough. In movie theaters, the close-up will appear on a big screen. If the thoughts and feelings are there, the audience will see them. So will the director, when he looks at the dailies a couple of days later on a full-scale screen. And no matter what he asked you to do during the shoot, he isn't going to appreciate overacting in his close-up. He may not love you on the day of shooting for resisting his suggestion, but he'll love you in dailies, and even more in the editing room when he's putting the film together, if you trust yourself and don't Act.

Jim Gandolfini told me that the first time he acted opposite John Travolta in *Get Shorty*, he couldn't see him acting at all—even from a few feet away. Travolta seemed not to be doing anything. But when Jim saw the film, there was plenty going on. And the camera had caught it all.

There are other aspects of the close-up that can make it difficult for the actor. Because the camera itself may be very close to him, he has to act to a mark—an X—taped onto the camera for the actor's eye-line. This odd situation is necessary in order to match the complex camera angles that for an audience mimic two actors talking to each other—when in fact the other actor may be saying his lines from an awkward or even unseen place off-camera. Odder still, sometimes there's no actor there at all. The lines are said by the script supervisor from behind the camera. In this situation, which happens frequently, you can't force your concentration. Instead, simply make yourself available to the line so you can let your imagination wander.

Show as little as possible. Let the line into you. Look at the X without staring. Let your mind and imagination take over. Take a breath in and out, and say the line. If you don't have a line, just listen.

When he was doing the remake of *Rear Window* after his accident, Christopher Reeve remembers, "The director wanted to get really close—a lot closer than I'm used to." Chris's character was supposed to be sitting at his window, looking at the people in the apartments across the street. But what he was actually looking at were two pieces of yellow tape on a black curtain. The actors who were to play the people in the apartments weren't even on set yet; their activities would be shot after dark. The director talked him through what was supposed to be happening. "Nothing could be more artificial," Chris recollects, "being told what was happening across the way and the imposition of the camera. I had to let that fuel my imagination rather than be inhibited by it. Thanks to all the work we'd done and to my life experience, none of that bothered me. I really didn't care. The emotional life was full because I was free."

At one moment, Chris recalls, "The camera is very, very close to me, and I am looking across the way. This beautiful girl is getting dressed to go out. At first I see her in her underwear, and there's a smile of appreciation. But then it changes to longing and sadness, because I'm in a wheelchair, and I could never be her partner or any woman's partner."

Even with the camera only a foot or two away, Reeve had been able to relax and access his emotions. His imagination had been set free by the sense that he "had nothing to lose," and didn't care whether he was being filmed. For him it was a breakthrough: "I don't think, when I look at it, that I got caught Acting in the movie." In fact, he got a Golden Globe nomination and his fellow actors voted him their Screen Actor's Guild Best Actor Award for this performance.

ACTING IN EPISODIC TELEVISION

Acting on television is basically the same as acting in film. However, there are some problems specific to television. Most of them have to do with time. An hour episode—almost the length of a feature film, really—is shot in seven to ten shooting days, as opposed to the six- to twelve-week schedule for a film. So more scenes must be shot each day than in feature film production, and the process tends to rush the actor even more. But rushing wastes time. It causes more mistakes, and it leads to routine acting—to obvious and melodramatic choices, comic choices that aren't funny, and over-pushed emotions.

Sometimes hurrying is the actor's response to the pressures of sustaining a successful series. Regarding his long-running role in *The Sopranos*, Jim Gandolfini says, "Sometimes you've gotta drum up all this shit all the time. You're like, Oh, Christ, here we go again. Especially if you're working a lot. You're like, If I just say it real fast, maybe they won't notice. Maybe they'll move on. But you can't do that." Rushing shows.

When I coach an actor for television, I'm forever slowing him down. My sense is that if I can get him to take his time at least for the two or three hours he is working with me, I'll have opened him up again to himself and his responses. I'll have reminded the actor to trust himself, and that reminder can stay with him. Then, even on camera, when the actor is being pushed to go fast, a piece of him will be saying, "Trust yourself. Take your time. Breathe. Explore."

Taking time to prepare in advance helps the actor to feel free and unpressured on the set. When James Gandolfini brought me the first episode of *The Sopranos* after our work on the pilot, I told him he would have to stay several days ahead of the shooting schedule in his memorizing and preparation if he wanted to be relaxed and available on camera. This much memorizing can be daunting at first. But it gets easier and quicker as you get into the routine of the show, especially if you continue to take the lines off the page properly. Getting to know the other actors and their characters helps. You will hear them in the lines as you go through the script. And when you are filming, all you have to do is listen, and your line will come to you in response.

Playing Major Roles on Episodic Television

Jim Gandolfini recalls that I helped him early on in our work together when I told him, "You don't have to know what a scene's about when you're doing it. Sometimes in real life you don't know what you really want or what you need." In episodic television, the major characters go through many episodes. The writers keep rewriting episodes and scenes, sometimes until the last moment before shooting begins. The actor doesn't always know how the story has changed from one week to the next or what will happen next. So it is best not to think about the story. Just go with the flow. Otherwise your effort to make sense of the story will show, and your acting will become repetitive, predictable, and melodramatic.

Even when you know exactly where the story is going, you must never *play* the story. To make a major character in episodic television multi-dimensional, you must play the moment. Respond to the lines, and let them take you through each change in the scene. By not playing the through-line of the scene, the actor lets the story play itself and opens up the greatest possibilities for character twists and surprises.

At the same time, a major actor in a series can't try to make every moment happen. If he does, he will wear himself out in a few episodes, and he will wear out the audience along with him. He must simply be available to the moment, without censoring himself or trying to make too much sense of it. There will always be another moment to stimulate him.

"You're the main character. Let the other actors come to you,"

Jim remembers me telling him. He elaborates, "I'm surrounded by great actors—Edie Falco, Lorraine Bracco, Michael Imperioli. I'm in awe of these people, the way they come in and do stuff. If I had tried to push it, to control the scenes—me, I'm swimming through muck, trying to figure out what to do. You said, 'Let them do their thing, and you just gotta be there and react.' "

Many of my students tell me they love Jim Gandolfini's acting because he's alive every moment on camera. They forget where he's coming from, and they can't guess where he's going. When I mention this to Jim, he says, 'That's because I probably don't know what I'm going to say next."

In one *Sopranos* episode, Tony gets angry at a telephone call and starts smashing the kitchen phone with the handset. Finally, he pulls the phone out of the wall. Jim told me that just before the take, he told Robert Iler, the actor who plays his son, to stand still. "I winged the thing this close to his head. I'm so glad it didn't hit him. It ended up in the dishwasher. That was all surprise. It's the best thing that happens." Surprises on set are not only good for the actor, they're good for the show. But the actor can't surprise the audience if he's thinking about what's going to happen next, or even what he's going to say next. You can't plan a surprise.

Acting is acting, whether in film, theater, or television. Except for these problems I've pointed out, an actor playing a major role on episodic television should be doing what he always does—finding the way to free himself from Acting, playing it moment by moment, letting his instinct and his emotions take him wherever they go, trusting the script to sculpt the character.

However, sometimes a young actor joining a series in a major role feels the pressure of his acting training weighing him down. Chris Noth told me about his work on *Law and Order*, which he had done before we started to work together. "It was a disastrous first year," he said. "This huge mountain of information—this technique that puts you in your head—makes you feel inadequate." He was talking about the techniques he had learned in acting school, which he was trying to apply to his episodic work on *Law and Order*. "I have to do all this stuff. If I don't do all these exercises my talent or instinct isn't going to catch on fire. I'm playing the history and pretty soon nothing is real. You're thinking about all that and the moment is escaping you. And on *Law and Order* I'm dealing with a text that's all procedure, indicated character references—truncated, staccato style."

Chris was on the show as a major character for several years. "But finally, I thought my best work was toward the end when I just didn't give a shit about that and I was playing the moment—being in the moment with the text. By that time I had done all the research, which didn't really kick in during the first year. But it did when I let it go, when I wasn't playing the work. I wasn't playing the research, I was playing the moment."

Guest Roles on Episodic Shows and Small Parts in Film

The biggest problem directors have with small parts in film or guest parts on television is that the actor playing the role wants to make a big impression. The actor wants to make a whole meal out of a snack. And when all the actors surrounding him are in a groove, an actor trying too hard to make a small role important will stick out even more.

Jim Gandolfini points out that playing small parts can be more demanding of the actor than a major or ongoing role. "Sometimes your character's got four or five scenes. He's there for a reason. So you've got to figure it out. 'Okay, what's this guy's life like?' It's not in the script. You've got to work ten times harder, cause it's not there. Tony Soprano is easy to play because it's there. I don't have to fill in the blanks. Every time I turn around, they're filled in. Sometimes it's harder to be the guy who comes in and is just there, has a few lines, and doesn't really have anything pushing him along."

With parts like this, it's important not to make a fuss about your acting. The way to do this, paradoxically, is to prepare as if the character were central to the series or film. Think of yourself as if you are on the show every week, or in the film throughout the entire shoot. Imagine that a given scene is just one of many in which you will act. Don't try to do too much. Talk to yourself before each take. Tell yourself, "I've been living this character. I know him better than anyone else. This is just another line, another thought, another moment in the character's life. So don't make it a big deal." You'll look more secure, and you'll act your best too.

So prepare as you would for any character. Anything you don't know, research or figure out. Let the lines, no matter how few, take you to your imagination. But do this, as always, instinctively. Don't struggle to be "imaginative"—just making up things about the character because you think you must. Let the character talk to you and let him take you wherever he goes.

Comic Roles

If you land a role in a sitcom, remember that like all acting it's about character. Yes, sitcoms have to be funny. You'll be told that by the director, the writer, the producer, the network executives, and your out-of-work actor friends. So you may be tempted to go for a big, silly, over-the-top style of acting in an attempt to please them quickly.

Don't. This approach will only make your acting general, whereas every successful character is funny in a specific way. True, sitcom acting can often be bigger than acting in dramatic series.

But the truly memorable sitcom actors have been memorable because their *characters*, not their acting per se, have been bigger, more outrageous, or extravagant—and utterly real. The audience won't find over-the-top acting funny, but a character that the audience *believes* is over the top may be funny.

For an actor to be funny in general, whether in sitcoms, film, or theater, he must be dead serious. Comic acting is about taking an assumption or idea to its illogical conclusion. It's Lucille Ball working in a chocolate factory, stuffing the chocolates into her mouth when the conveyor belt goes too fast for her to pack them. It's illogical to us but completely logical to Lucy. She has been told that, above all, she must not let the chocolates fall off the end of the belt or she'll be fired. So when she can't keep up, she eats one chocolate, then another and another. Those she can't cram into her mouth she puts in her bra. She can't swallow. She starts to get sick. But she stuffs her mouth with more and more chocolates because she doesn't want to be fired.

If a moment is illogical to the audience but logical to the character, it will be both true and funny. The more illogical to the audience and the more logical to the character, the funnier it will be.

GETTING TO BIG EMOTIONAL MOMENTS

For young actors, big emotional moments, whether on stage or in film or television, can be daunting. This is because of their fear that the emotion won't be there when they need it and the distraction of what they think is expected of them. So they push for a bigger feeling than they need, which makes things worse. I know because I've been there. I found it hard to be as emotional on stage as I was in life when I was a young actor. And all the exercises to free my emotions only exacerbated the fear of not having them in performance.

What I have been striving for in this book is to help young actors attack their fears by placing their concentration on what really matters—being in the moment without censoring yourself—in order to access instinct and emotion. This process gets easier as you get older, simply because for most of us, the older we get, the less we care about what is expected of us. When we do what interests us and what we really want, our emotions come along for the ride. They are a natural by-product of listening and responding. I don't believe an actor needs to do anything special most of the time for his emotions to be available to him. And whatever feelings arise in him can be used for the character.

Every actor finds his own way to get to his emotions in tight spots. Glenn Close put it vividly when she said, "Actors are like car radios. You put 'seek' on, and we go back and forth and back and forth until we home in on something that will elicit a response. We're all emotional station seekers." It doesn't matter how we hit the emotion, as long as we are open to the script and to ourselves—not only our memories but our imaginations.

For me, surprise is a major element. In each take, I go to a different place, to surprise myself, to see what happens. Sometimes I'll yell in inappropriate places or take a pause where it doesn't belong. If it doesn't work, I always have another take and another surprise. I remind myself to be bold in the take, not to try to sneak into the emotion. If you have prepared well, this is the time to take your chances—to go somewhere new, do something different, shock yourself.

There are times, however, when we have to get to a big emotional moment quickly. In the theater this is not so difficult. Usually a play develops in a sequential way for the character, so the actor's feelings build naturally to even big emotional moments if he concentrates on what he hears and says, moment by moment. His natural response to the text will take him to his feelings, as long as he doesn't care what feelings come up. If, however, the actor is preoccupied with the emotion he believes he must reach later in the scene, he will be distracted by it and unable to concentrate on the present moment. He will no longer be listening or responding, and his fears will take over. He will find himself with no emotion. Then he will try to push his feelings, and that's what the audience will see.

And in film and television, when we don't have the luxury of performing in sequence, we can't always rely on the script alone to provoke our feelings. Sometimes, for technical reasons, even a given scene will not be shot from beginning to end. For instance, if a scene starts in the bedroom and continues down the stairs, through the living room, into the kitchen, and then back up into the bedroom, the beginning and end will be shot first, to accommodate the camera and crew. So in movies, emotions frequently can't be carried through. And the actor may have to be able to get quickly to an emotion—particularly a big one—especially for a close-up.

I'm not a big believer in exercises for actors, but I have developed one as an aid for the actor who, after thinking about a scene and preparing it, feels compelled to explore the lines with a deeper emotion or to go to a very big emotion. Jim Gandolfini refers to it as The Breathing Thing. Here's how it goes:

Take a quick breath in and hold it. Contract and release your diaphragm in a very fast rhythm, so that it feels as if it is vibrating. The sensation will be like a fast panting. Let your entire chest start to shake. This allows your solar plexus, which is in the center of your chest between the left and right ribs, to shake as well. Let your mind wander—picking up whatever memories, images, or thoughts come to you in relation to the scene you're playing and the emotion you're exploring. Your held breath should feel stuck in the vibration, as if you cannot expel it easily. The sensation may remind you of what you felt like as a child in the grip of a sobbing fit, your diaphragm contracting spasmodically and your breath caught up in it. The images may keep changing. Different faces or experiences may surface, remembered or imagined. Imagine yourself growing chilled, cold, even freezing. It doesn't matter how odd the shaking becomes as long as you do it.

Continue until you must have air. Then let out your breath and begin the exercise again. Repeat for twenty minutes, no more. You may be surprised at how quickly the feelings come upon you. Within a very short time, you may be crying or raging. When that happens, stop! You are finished for the night, even if it's only taken you five minutes.

Here's what happens to me one evening when I do The Breathing Thing:

I take a breath and let my diaphragm begin to vibrate very fast. My mother's face comes to me. I keep the shaking in my chest going. I see her at my father's funeral, pushing his casket so that it gently rocks back and forth on the canvas ropes that are ready to lower him into the grave.

I let my breath out and begin again: quick breath, hold it, diaphragm shaking. My mother's face comes to me in her shroud, in her simple casket. I can't breathe, so I let the air out.

With the next breath, the shaking comes very fast. I am cold. My mother's sweet face comes to me like a sleeping, swaddled baby's. I see my grandmother's face in hers, my uncles' faces. I have seen these images before but the exercise makes them come one upon the other, flooding me with emotion. I can't hold back. I let my feelings up the back of my ears into my sinuses, and into my eyes. I let the tears fall. I don't judge whether it's enough tears.

I take a few moments to let myself breathe naturally, to let the image go. When I am breathing calmly, I am finished with the exercise.

At first you may be distracted by the technical aspects of the process until you get used to the breathing. You may also find that you get mildly light-headed as you do the exercise. That's as it should be. The exercise works by changing your natural breathing pattern, bypassing the usual distanced responses to go quickly to the feelings we have when we are startled by an image or thought that has real emotional power—the strong emotions we associate with the state of bodily agitation we have artificially created. The shaking prolongs and intensifies the feeling and won't let you get away from it. In other words, the exercise throws the actor into a physiological state that reflexively generates the intense images, thoughts, and emotions that would typically have brought on that state in the first place, and that are indelibly associated with it in our deepest being.

"It throws everything off," Jim Gandolfini says about The Breathing Thing. "When you do it, you can go a lot of places really quick. It helped me because when I'm doing *The Sopranos*, sometimes I literally only have time to change clothes before I have to go to a scene where I have to get angry." Jim does The Breathing Thing in his trailer, and reports, "You get angry real quick."

Bernadette Peters uses The Breathing Thing not only in film, but in concert. She told me, "When I have to change moods quickly—go to an emotional song, an emotional place, a place I know I want to be—during the intro to the next song, I turn away from the audience and do The Breathing Thing to prepare myself. It wakes things up!"

In order to get comfortable with this exercise, you should do it every night over a period of several weeks. Pick a different emotion each night, unless you're already filming. In that case, use the emotion coming from the scene. Even then, don't feel obliged to stick with that emotion. Let your mind wander to whatever feeling comes up. And don't obsess about doing the exercise perfectly. There is no exact "right way"—everyone does it his own way.

Don't judge the success of the exercise by how much you cry or how big the feeling is. You must never judge your feelings because you'll never think they are enough. Then you will do too much. The next night, do the exercise again. Maybe nothing will happen. That's all right. Work on it for twenty minutes, then stop, even if nothing has happened. Go back the next night and try it again.

Once you get familiar with this exercise, you can use it to kick-start your emotions for a particular scene. Go through the exercise for twenty minutes each evening in the period leading up to shooting. On the day of the shoot, begin the exercise right before going on set, but stop just when the emotion starts to push through. Then forget about it. You want to take yourself up to the moment of release, as if you were priming a pump, then leave the surprise to happen in front of the camera. When you are on camera, don't do anything special—just play the scene. You will probably find the emotion popping up on you in different places. Let it happen. Don't try to control it. You have primed yourself, so it will happen on its own. However, if the emotion isn't there on the take, do the exercise in front of the camera during the take. That is, start the shaking. Let your mind wander. Imagine the cold. Let the feeling surface from behind your ears into your sinuses. Let it out almost as if you are going to fake it—but don't fake it. Fill it with yourself and it will be there.

This is not a trick. The thoughts and feelings are yours. Disorienting your breathing is just another way to attack your fear of not having a "real" feeling by allowing your feelings to arise. But you can't get there just because you're supposed to, because you've been told to cry or get angry. You have to have done the work to under-stand the scene and to explore it in a personal way. You must be-lieve and want your reaction; it must matter to you.

Let me close this chapter with an experience I had coaching on set.

Aaliyah had come to study acting with me when she was nine-teen years old and already a rhythm-and-blues recording star with two platinum albums to her credit. Even though she had never acted before, I could see she had a natural talent, ferocious drive, and discipline. I also knew she would be cast in films quickly. So we worked together three or more times a week on scenes and monologues from Chekhov and Shakespeare, along with Sam Shepard and other contemporary playwrights. She was by nature shy and gentle, so I worked on getting her to express rage and other big feelings.

As I had expected, within six months Aaliyah was cast to play the leading role opposite Jet Li in *Romeo Must Die*. Joel Silver, the producer, and Andrzej Bartkoviak, the director, asked me to come on set in Vancouver to coach both Aaliyah and Jet.

We had a couple of weeks before filming began. I worked with each actor privately every day for a few hours, going through the whole script in sequence, as well as rehearsing with the director and other cast members.

The character Aaliyah was playing was feisty, fun, loving, smart, witty, serious, and angry. In the script, she was called on to play two scenes that would have challenged any actress. In one scene, she sees her dead brother being taken to the morgue in a body bag after he has been thrown out of the window of a high-rise and accuses her father of being responsible for his death. In the other scene, she tells Jet's character a story about her brother and herself as children and then reveals to him that her brother has been killed. The second scene was going to be shot quite early in the filming. So while working Aaliyah through the script as a whole, I also had her preparing emotionally for that scene.

Aaliyah was close to her family and had a lot of emotion about them to call on. She had a brother whom she adored, so we discussed her fears for him. Then we spent time on The Breathing Thing, getting down into the emotion. At first it was difficult for her to let go completely. She would always get to a truthful and touching place, but at first she couldn't pop the feeling. I was not surprised. After all, she was a young actress in her first film. Her days were filled with costume fittings, make-up tests, camera tests, rehearsals, and rewrites. Everything was moving fast, except for the few hours we had together each day when she could really work on the role.

Soon the scene with Jet was nearly upon us. Three days before, we started focusing more intensively on that scene in addition to the material she was shooting each day. The night before the shoot for that scene, we went over it again. Aaliyah was worried because she still didn't feel entirely free emotionally.

I knew we were in for a long day, but I had confidence in Aaliyah's talent. My chief concern was that, given the pressure, she might push her emotions. Or she might go for the emotion too early, using it up before the time the close-up came.

Early the next morning, we met on the set, a small room. I didn't work the scene with her at first, assuring her that we had plenty of time. First there would be a rehearsal to set the camera and lighting, then the initial shots—a master and a two-shot favoring Jet. I told Aaliyah we didn't need to have it all for those. After the rehearsal, we went to a quiet place to prepare the scene for the shots being set up.

The story Aaliyah's character tells Jet's is about a prank she and her brother played on their mother when they were children. She pretended her brother had collapsed and ran to their mother for help. When the mother came, he jumped up and surprised her. The prank scared their mother so much that she burst into tears and scolded both of them. At that point in the story, Aaliyah's character breaks down, revealing to Jet the truth: "They killed him. They killed my beautiful brother."

I had Aaliyah do The Breathing Thing: take a breath, hold it, let the breath start to shake her body, feel the cold, let her mind wander into loss, see her brother, keep shaking, hold the breath until she couldn't, then expel the air and start again. After a few minutes, I stopped her. "Good," I said. "But I didn't get there," she said desperately. "Right," I answered, "not yet. We have a long way to go."

Aaliyah went out and played the scene through the master shot. They did a bunch of takes, and she was good in all of them. After the master shot, the crew changed the lighting for the medium shots favoring Jet. This took a couple of hours. During that time, I kept her with me and apart from the crew so she wouldn't fritter away her energy. We talked about a lot of things.

The medium shots went well too. Jet and Aaliyah were still just getting to know each other, but he seemed touched by her acting. There were three cameras on them. One was a medium shot on Aaliyah. The whole set was growing very tense, as it often does when someone has a highly emotional scene to play. Sometimes it can make the pressure on the actor intolerable.

We had another two-hour wait during the set-up for the close-ups. Aaliyah and I spent the time together talking. I told her about some violent experiences of mine that caused rage in me; she talked of her grandmother's illness, her fears for her father, her brother; I talked about my mother at my father's funeral. We talked through many different experiences. I must have cried ten times. But Aaliyah was too afraid to cry yet. I took her into The Breathing Thing but again stopped her before she was finished.

We were called to the set. I talked with Jet, whom I had also been coaching throughout the day. They did a rehearsal for camera and lighting. One camera was a medium shot on Aaliyah, another was a close-up on her, and a third a close-up on Jet. I asked the director to shoot the rehearsal in case it was the best take. He did. It was a good take but not quite as good as I thought it would get.

Everything was set for Aaliyah's close-up. I checked with the director to be sure. With such a big scene and such a young actress, we didn't want to risk losing the take for technical reasons if she was there emotionally.

I went behind the couch Aaliyah was sitting on and leaned over so that no one could hear what I said.

"Take a breath."

She did.

"Hold it," I said. "Go down into yourself, see your beautiful brother, let it shake out of you."

She did.

Then I said, "Just tell the story simply, like a little girl. But when you get to the line, 'They killed him. They killed my beautiful brother,' yell it! I want you to yell it so loud you scare the crap out of Jet."

"What?" she said, panicking. "You never told me to do that before."

"I know," I said. "Just do it. Scream at him. Scare yourself. Scream it!"

I left. She was shaking, but I knew she could handle it. She was strong and prepared.

"Action" was called. Aaliyah started the scene. She told the story. She was obviously upset, but she kept going. She was simple and beautiful, as if distracted by some terrible truth. Then all of a sudden, surprising herself and all of us watching, she yelled at Jet fiercely, "They killed my brother!" Her rage burst and her tears came flying out. "My beautiful brother." She finished the lines in tears, just like a little girl—she was so lost, so young, so heartbroken.

The director called, "Cut. Print." We all rushed to Aaliyah. She asked, "Was it all right?"

"Yeah, it was all right," I said. "It was more than all right."

Jet's take was great too because he had allowed himself simply to respond to Aaliyah's acting.

The director and producer were thrilled and relieved. "We got it," Andrzej said. "Let's go home."

I was so proud of this remarkable young actress. And I use this story as an example because I knew Aaliyah was at the point a lot of talented young actors are at when they are faced with a big emotional moment. She was prepared. She had the feelings in her, and she was in touch with them and with the scene. But her fear that she wouldn't get to an emotional peak could easily have gotten in the way. She needed one last piece of the puzzle to go the distance: she needed to surprise herself in order to put herself on the edge. She needed to be unsure of what to do and confused enough not to give a damn where she went.

I gave Aaliyah the surprise, but you can learn to give it to yourself. You must do the best preparation you can, and then trust yourself enough to go someplace you don't know in front of the camera. Go to the unknown and discover it at the moment. Your instinct will take you to the best you have to offer.

Aaliyah did only one other film, for which I helped her prepare, although I could not be on set with her. She died in a plane crash before we got an opportunity to tape a conversation about our work together. I miss working on the great plays with her, and on the many film roles she would have inhabited so intimately.

6

"It's what Hamlet was saying to the Players, 'Don't over-do it, but don't under-do it either.' I suppose a more refined definition of acting is hitting it just right. It's just perfect, but it's not perfection. It's knowing when to leave it alone, to finesse it, throw it away. Or when to make a meal of it. It's instinctive."

—Kevin Kline

We usually think of the great roles—Hamlet, Lear, Viola, Ophelia, Othello, Desdemona—as the point an actor's career builds toward, the ultimate test of his talent and skill. And they are. But the big, multidimensional roles also offer the most important lessons in conceiving and developing character for actors at all stages of their training and growth. They force us to give up trying to control the character and let the character play us. They expose our acting tricks, the gimmicks we do with our voices, bodies, and emotions—including those for which we have been praised in the past. They expose especially the tricks we do with dialogue—substituting facile line readings for simple truths, and dramatizing our emotions rather than letting them surface instinctively.

The great roles require our all, and then some. Playing Hamlet, for instance, you can't just play your idea of Hamlet. You have to bring all your experiences in life—all your rage, love, passion, and sensitivity, as well as all your intelligence, knowledge, and powers of concentration. And even that may not be enough. We must become bigger people to become big enough for such a role. And that is the paramount challenge and joy of acting.

BUILDING EMOTIONAL RANGE

The great roles build emotional range. This is why I work on the classical repertoire with beginning actors, and why, in 1987, I created the Classical Workshop at the New York Shakespeare Festival. The idea of the Workshop was to introduce actors to Shakespeare and other classic plays as well as to take actors with classical experience through roles they had not yet played. Aidan Quinn would come in to explore Marc Antony in *Julius Caesar*, or Peter Coyote to explore Cassius, or Kevin Kline and Phoebe Cates to try Romeo and Juliet.

I developed one- and two-week workshops in which actors started with sonnets to become comfortable with verse, moved on to soliloquies of characters they might play someday, and then tackled complicated scenes with other actors. Actors would spend four hours each day in small groups, immersing themselves in Shakespeare's language and exploring his characters. It was quite an experience to watch Sally Field attacking the role of Hermione in *The Winter's Tale*; Diane Wiest approaching Lady Macbeth as a loving wife rather than the harridan she is so often portrayed as; Goldie Hawn finding the simplicity and truth in a sonnet; Joel Grey, as a charming, scary Richard III, seducing a weeping young woman whose husband he has killed; Cicely Tyson as Gertrude describing the death of Ophelia in *Hamlet*; Kris Kristofferson plumbing the depths of Macbeth's soliloquy "Tomorrow and tomorrow and tomorrow." The richness of exploring Shakespeare took all these actors—even the most experienced of them—to new places, giving them new insights into the human condition as well as their own acting. They responded to the work as if they had come upon an acting oasis where they could replenish themselves on Shakespeare's profound language.

When I worked with Glenn Close on Cleopatra, the text illuminated a sensuality in her that I had not seen before. She was funny, coy, petulant, irritating, angry, spoiled, sexy, loving, and profoundly in touch with great loss. The brilliance of Shakespeare's dialogue allowed Glenn to explore this complex character in depth even in the short time we had in the Workshop. Although she has not yet performed this role on stage or screen, audiences have seen the qualities she discovered in many of the roles she has since played in films—the Marquise de Merteuil in *Dangerous Liaisons*, the erotically predatory young editor with whom Michael Douglas gets involved in *Fatal Attraction*, her Gertrude in Franco Zeffirelli's film of *Hamlet*, Sunny von Bulow in *Reversal of Fortune*.

You will find it valuable to work on great characters on your own, even if you don't get a chance to play them in performance. They will make you a more powerful actor and put you more deeply in touch with your feelings, even uncovering hidden aspects of your personality. They will open you to the best and worst within you, and that will help you to grow as both an actor and a human being.

To play Hamlet, you must be not only the beautiful, intelligent, clever prince, but also the grotesque, crafty, vulgar madman. Ophelia says of Hamlet:

Now see that noble and most sovereign reason,
Like sweet bells jangled, out of time and harsh;
That unmatched form and feature of blown youth
Blasted with ecstasy.

And indeed he is violent and hateful to his mother. He is touched by the old Player at one moment, full of self-loathing the next. He is a consummate fencer who kills Polonius and Laertes with regret, but he is also the vicious murderer who kills Claudius without remorse.

Nor is he without humor. Hamlet can be and is funny, although his humor is often dark. He is witty as well as crafty and cruel with Rosencrantz and Guildenstern, whom he knows are betraying him to Claudius, and he makes a number of jokes at the expense of Polonius, as when he answers the foolish question, "What do you read, my lord?" with a literal, "Words, words, words." When Kevin Kline played Hamlet, he played this scene sitting quite strangely, as if on a chair with one leg crossed over the other and a book on his lap—but there was no chair. He answered, while continuing to read, "Words, words . . . " There was a pause as Kevin continued reading, then he turned the page and said, "Words." The change in rhythm made the audience laugh. It also highlighted the humor and brilliance of this famous line.

To play a man of as many parts as Hamlet, an actor must give himself up to the text and let it take him wherever it goes.

The Role of Imagination

The great roles will help you to explore who you are, but you will not find there enough to fill the role. If you try to limit these characters to what you already know and feel, you will be too small to inhabit them. If you are to do justice to them, you must fly up to them—rather than dragging them down to you—by expanding your range of knowledge and strengthening your imagination. Your imagination must become as real and important to you as your memories and feelings. So you must be willing to study things you do not yet know, and you must study them in such depth that *what you study becomes you.* What you take into yourself about human behavior, politics, sociology, the history of the Middle Ages and the Renaissance, and so on, will allow you to reach places in yourself you didn't know existed before. No line, no image, no thought can be left general. You must understand and feel each one in a specific and personal way. Your work on the text and character will not be complete until this is so.

This process takes time, concentration, and creativity. When you read about an earlier era in a novel or a history book, you must let your imagination take over. See yourself there, in that period. It's not enough, when acting, to wear the costume—you must be able to imagine yourself in the moment on stage in a way that is real to you. So you must immerse yourself not only in the play but also in history as a real, living study. Read about the politics, art, music, dance, and customs of the period. Look at its art in museums and listen to its music in concerts and on recordings.

Against Interpretation

It is fashionable now to have an "idea" of how to play these great characters—an interpretation: Hamlet as an intellectual and therefore unable to make a decision or act impulsively; Hamlet in Oedipal terms, preoccupied with his fixation on his mother and therefore unable to avenge his father's murder. But a one-note interpretation of a character is the opposite of the kind of imaginative, wide-ranging search for knowledge I have been describing. Any single idea you have will illuminate an aspect of the character at best. It will be too small, too limiting, for the character as a whole.

These parts are rounded human beings who emerge from rich texts. We must know as much about them as possible. But we must also let them come alive in the playwright's hands; we must let them move from line to line and moment to moment without shackling them to a narrow interpretation. After all, real human beings react with more choices, thoughts, emotions, and changes than any actor, no matter how brilliant, can think of. So we must allow these great characters every opportunity to be real. Critics and audiences may analyze the performance afterwards and praise or fault our "interpretation." But we, as actors, must not interpret. We must give ourselves—including our intellect—over to the role, and let the text take us where it will.

Actors may believe that an interpretation puts their personal stamp on the role, but it actually does the reverse. It not only diminishes the character, it makes the character less personal because the interpretation comes from the intellect, and intellect is only a part of us. And although really good actors are intelligent, it's a different kind of intelligence—not so much analytical as instinctive. To make the character a full human being, the actor needs all of himself—his mind, his instinct, his imagination, his personal experiences, and the whole range of his responses to the text, not only in preparation but alive in performance.

I believe the real reason actors try to play an "idea"—an interpretation—is because they want to control the character. That is why they are willing to limit the possibilities and choices. But the actor can't really control anything when he acts, except maybe the possibility that he be truly present every moment he is on stage. And there is no better way to learn this than by playing these roles.

Using the Negative

What makes the great roles daunting, in addition to their inherent depth and complexity, is the fact that they have been played by important actors again and again and again. Every actor who comes to the major classical and modern repertoire has in his head Olivier's Hamlet, Henry V, and Richard III, Richard Burton's Becket, Katharine Hepburn's Mary in Eugene O'Neill's *Long Day's Journey into Night*, and Marlon Brando's Stanley in *A Streetcar Named Desire*, among other memorable performances. It is necessary for the actor to approach such roles from the negative, saying to himself, "Anything but what I remember from that particular performance."

When Kevin Kline was cast as Henry V for the 1984 New York Shakespeare Festival at the Delacorte Theatre in Central Park, he and I were both more than familiar with Lawrence Olivier's monumental portrayal of Henry V in the film version of the play. Olivier's Henry V, with his crisp, heroic speech, had seemed the perfect king for World War II, when the film was made, and the portrayal was still resonant in the 1960s and 1970s when Kevin and I first saw it. But Kevin had the sound of Olivier's Henry still whizzing through his head at maximum speed.

The first thing he did was to slow down his own speech. He pulled each line apart simply to make sense of it, allowing the language to become clear and resonant for him. Kevin wanted his Henry to be personal and very human, as opposed to Olivier's confident King. Olivier's Henry didn't seem to have any doubts about himself or his position. Kevin saw him as full of uncertainty.

After all, we had been through the Vietnam War and were instinctively suspicious of what looked like jingoistic clichés in the play. So we talked about John F. Kennedy as a possible model for the character—the scion of a powerful, wealthy family, groomed from boyhood to be president. Henry V's father, Henry IV, was powerful but distant; there were suspicions about his right to the throne. John F. Kennedy's father, Joe Kennedy, had served as Ambassador to England but never overcame a certain political dubiousness. Although Henry spends most of his youth with common men—Falstaff and his group of drunks, lechers, and thieves—he asserts his nobility when he goes to war for his father and defeats Hotspur, a true nobleman in the earlier history plays. He had the "common touch," but also the "touch of a prince." Many felt the same of JFK.

But Kevin was not using Kennedy as an interpretation. Rather, he was invoking Kennedy as an inspiration, to get him in touch with his own thoughts and feelings about the kind of king he himself would like to be—a king in touch with real people and their feelings, dreams, passions, and fears.

In Act IV, scene 3, Henry addresses his weary troops before the battle of Agincourt. They are outnumbered ten to one by a fresh and confident French army. As Henry approaches, he hears Westmoreland:

> O! that we now had here
> But one ten thousand of those men in England,
> That do no work to-day!

King Henry begins:

> What's he that wishes so?
> My cousin Westmoreland? No, my fair cousin:
> If we are mark'd to die, we are enow [enough]
> To do our country loss; and if to live,
> The fewer men, the greater share of honor.

Olivier had delivered this speech as a classic piece of bravura acting, starting simply and building piece by piece to a rousing call to war. Kevin did the opposite. He started by raging the first line, "What's he that wishes so?" Having startled everyone, he paused a bit, then he broke the silence:

> My cousin Westmoreland? No, my fair cousin:
> If we are mark'd to die, we are enow
> To do our country loss; and if to live,
> The fewer men, the greater share of honor.

Kevin's voice got louder and louder, line by line—a crescendo of outrage, increasing with each thought until, almost shouting, he bellowed:

> O! do not wish one more:
> Rather proclaim it, Westmorland, through my host,
> That he which hath no stomach to this fight,
> Let him depart . . .
> We would not die in that man's company
> That fears his fellowship to die with us.

Then he stopped. He took a long pause as he looked around at his men. When their surprise and his anger subsided, he said simply, quietly, as if he were only just realizing what day it was, "This day is called the Feast of Crispian." Then he continued, more personally:

> He that outlives this day, and comes safe home,
> Will stand a tip-toe when this day is named,
> And rouse him at the name of Crispian.

Then he got more and more personal, describing what it would be like in years to come for those men who survive this battle and celebrate the feast of Saint Crispian in England. Then with deep emotion, face to face with each man in turn, he said very slowly and quietly:

We few, we happy few, we band of brothers:
For he today that sheds his blood with me
Shall be my brother.

I am still touched, remembering this moment. Kevin's Henry seemed truly to offer his men his brotherhood—the brotherhood of a king. Man to man, shedding blood together. He and they were one; he asked them to fight on personal terms, as partners. And he got quieter and more personal as the speech progressed, rather than more and more heroic.

There are examples of great actors in the past using this negative approach to the Great Roles. Olivier rejected Gielgud's beautifully spoken, sensitive, classical Hamlet which was so popular in his day for a swift, modern, psychologically complex Hamlet. He said he just wanted to make it contemporary. Olivier's Othello was a mixture of sensuality and primal animal fierceness as opposed to the earlier renowned Othello of Paul Robeson that was all nobility. We see this again and again with great actors rejecting former portrayals of these roles in order to be free to re-create them. These roles are so capacious they allow for infinite variations. They contain multitudes.

DEALING WITH SHAKESPEARE'S LANGUAGE

To act Shakespeare, an actor must be verbal. From the tinkers in *A Midsummer Night's Dream* to Hamlet, all of Shakespeare's characters express themselves in words textured with description and allusion. So the actor must be able to express himself using their words.

When the actor is able to speak such rich language with ease and authenticity, the effect can be unforgettable. I remember, for example, a production of *Twelfth Night* that Joseph Papp asked me to direct for the New York Shakespeare Festival in Central Park. I'd immediately thought of Mary Elizabeth Mastrantonio for the role of Viola. She was a beautiful, intelligent young actress, deeply emotional yet fiery and tough minded—all qualities needed for the role. And having coached her for many years, I knew she wouldn't be intimidated by Viola's poetic dialogue.

It was a startling performance. Because of her freedom with the dialogue, Mary Elizabeth was able to create a brilliant, poetic, sassy character who never lost her femininity, and yet was totally believable and charming as a young man in male clothing. The depth of her emotion popped up in surprising and illuminating ways. One moment in particular stands out in my memory. Viola, impersonating the Duke's page, delivers a message of love to the veiled Countess Olivia, played by Michelle Pfeiffer. Since she herself is in love with the Duke, she is irritated by Olivia's rejection of him; she cannot understand why any woman would spurn this wonderful man. Viola says, "Good madam, let me see your face." Mary Elizabeth said this as a challenge, as if she were saying, "Remove your veil, so I can see what the hell the Duke is so hot about."

After protesting, Olivia says, "We will draw the curtain and show you the picture." When she let the veil drop, Mary Elizabeth looked at Olivia's face, and everything stopped. Her own face said it all: the Duke is in love with this image of beauty and femininity. I am a boy in the Duke's eyes. I can't compete with that. How can I ever have his love as a woman? Tears came to her eyes and she looked away. It was a stunning moment.

There was a pause. Olivia, unsure of why Viola turned away, became vulnerable, confused, hurt. She asked simply, "Is't not well done?"

Mary Elizabeth answered truthfully, even humbly, "Excellently done." She took a moment to gather herself and then said, wickedly, "*If God did all.*" The audience roared with laughter. Her sudden shift from a deep sense of loss to this feisty, sharp wit created a marvelous surprise.

If Shakespeare's language offers some of the greatest possibilities to the actor, however, it can also pose one of the greatest obstacles, particularly when the lines are in verse. On top of our reflexive tendency to artificially heighten our inflection when we see lines as verse, there are the endless debates about what a "proper" Shakespearian delivery should be.

We don't really know how the lines were spoken in Shakespeare's time, but even if we did, how useful is some generalized "Shakespearian" style of speaking and acting? Each play is set in a different time and place, and each character comes from a specific class, period, and location. The specifics of time and place and their attendant styles are enormously important, as are each character's specific lines. So how can we have a general style for speaking Shakespeare's lines?

Of course we should study the history of Shakespeare's time—the political, social, and literary history as well as the language and poetry. As actors, we should know as much as possible. And we should study speech and voice. It broadens our range and offers us possibilities. But in the end, it is the specific play and character that matters to us, not any general notion of how the lines may have been spoken or the plays performed in Shakespeare's time.

I know that the model for acting Shakespeare is British acting. And there are great British actors whose work I admire. But I don't believe they should be a model for American actors. The manner of speaking English in England today is no closer to the way Shakespeare spoke four hundred years ago than our manner of speaking in the United States.

I believe we have to forget about "style" in speaking and acting and go back to the text. The text is the source. It gives us the character. Make the character alive, a breathing human being, and the play will come alive. If the audience is to believe the character, the actor must treat the lines as realistic dialogue, speaking them with as little fuss about the poetry as possible. If the phrase or line is poetic, so be it. It doesn't need the actor to make it beautiful. If it is written as poetry, and the actor says the lines simply, the lines will be both real and poetic. But if the actor becomes too conscious of his beautiful speech, he will likely forget what he is saying—the sound of his voice will smother the simple truth of the line and its personal meaning for the actor.

The actor can begin by pulling the lines apart, stopping to find out exactly what each word means. Use a Shakespeare glossary or dictionary—I use Alexander Schmidt's *Shakespeare Lexicon and Quotation Dictionary*, or for quick reference, C. T. Onions's *A Shakespeare Glossary*, which is more compact. Then try to take the line or phrase off the page. If a word or phrase feels foreign to you, so that you feel as if you're translating as you say it, stop. Replace the word or phrase with a modern equivalent and try it again.

JULIET. Gallop apace, you fiery-footed steeds, Towards
    Phoebus lodging!

In Act III, scene 2 of *Romeo and Juliet*, Juliet is waiting for Romeo. They were secretly married in the morning, and now in the afternoon she is waiting for night to come so that she and Romeo can be together.

Take the first line off the page, looking up any words you don't know.

Gallop apace: gallop quickly.
You fiery-footed steeds: horses that draw the chariot of the sun
   god or the sun itself.
Towards Phoebus lodging: Phoebus Apollo is the sun god; his
   lodging, where he sleeps, is where the sun sets in the west.

Juliet is looking up at the sun and ordering it to move more quickly to where it sets.

After saying the line, repeat it in your own words: "Gallop quickly to where the sun sets, you fiery-footed horses." Then go back to the original lines. Go back and forth between your words and Shakespeare's until the words, thoughts, and image are really coming from your mouth.

This can take time, but until an actor truly means what he says, he can't be in the moment.

Sometimes Shakespeare's phrasing trips up actors. Verbs aren't always where we expect them to be, either for poetic reasons or because of historical differences in speech. If the phrasing is giving you a problem, rearrange the phrase or sentence so that it reverberates as modern speech. Then go back and forth between your phrasing and Shakespeare's until you truly mean the line the way he wrote it.

In Act II, scene 2 of *Romeo and Juliet*, Juliet has been surprised by Romeo on the balcony while voicing her love for him to the night air. She says to him:

Thou knowest the mask of night is on my face,
Else would a maiden blush bepaint my cheek
For that which thou hast heard me speak tonight.

Take the lines off the page, looking up words you do not know and rearranging phrases to make them accessible to you.

Thou knowest: you know
The mask of night: the cover of darkness
Is on my face: is hiding my face

So, in contemporary English we say: "You know the cover of darkness is hiding my face."

Else: otherwise
would a maiden blush: a virgin blush, an embarrassed blush
bepaint my cheek: be painted on my cheek

In contemporary English this becomes: "Otherwise my cheeks would be painted with a virgin blush of embarrassment."

Keep going back and forth between the contemporary phrasing and Shakespeare's until you can say them with equal freedom and meaning. Stop yourself when you are not meaning what you say. Use the modern word or phrase and then go back to pure Shakespeare.

Be patient. The process is worth the time it takes, because you will never get more exciting or deeper material to work on. Once you get past the first stage, you won't feel the need to Act.

Suggestions for Working on Your Own with Shakespeare

Men should start with Sonnet 130:

My mistress' eyes are nothing like the sun,
Coral is far more red than her lips' red.
If snow be white, why then her breasts are dun;
If hairs be wires, black hairs grow on her head.
I have seen roses damasked, red and white,
But no such roses see I in her cheeks;
And in some perfumes is there more delight
Than in the breath that from my mistress reeks.
I love to hear her speak, yet well I know
That music hath a far more pleasing sound.
I grant I never saw a goddess go:
My mistress when she walks treads on the ground.
*   And yet, by heaven, I think my love as rare*
*   As any she belied with false compare.*

Women should start with Sonnet 57:

Being your slave, what should I do but tend
Upon the hours and times of your desire?
I have no precious time at all to spend,
Nor services to do, till you require.
Nor dare I chide the world-without-end hour
Whilst I, my sovereign, watch the clock for you,
Nor think the bitterness of absence sour
When you have bid your servant once adieu.
Nor dare I question with my jealous thought
Where you may be, or your affairs suppose,

But like a sad slave stay and think of naught
Save, where you are, how happy you make those.
*   So true a fool is love that in your will,*
*   Though you do anything, he thinks no ill.*

Even though this is poetry with rhymes and all, don't think of it that way. Deal with each line as if it is a line of dialogue. Take each line off the page in pieces, looking up any words you don't know. Don't worry about understanding the whole sonnet as you work. Instead, let each phrase into your head and allow it to make sense in itself. Say it simply. Whatever the line means to you at that moment, say it with your own feelings.

Gradually, you will become aware that this short series of lines is making sense to you and creating feelings in you. It will also allow you to become comfortable with Shakespeare's phrasing and vocabulary as well as his imagery. Don't try to be poetic, and don't panic about not understanding the sonnet at first. Be patient, work in pieces, and it will come to you.

After spending at least a few days exploring the first sonnet, try another. Men and women both should find Sonnet 29 interesting and rich to work on.

When in disgrace with fortune and men's eyes,
I all alone beweep my outcast state,
And trouble deaf heaven with my bootless cries,
And look upon myself and curse my fate,
Wishing me like to one more rich in hope,
Featured like him, like him with friends possessed,
Desiring this man's art and that man's scope,
With what I most enjoy contented least:
Yet in these thoughts myself almost despising,
Haply I think on thee, and then my state,

Like the lark at break of day arising
From sullen earth, sings hymns at heaven's gate;
*   For thy sweet love remembered such wealth brings*
*   That then I scorn to change my state with kings.*

After working on these two sonnets, you may want to continue with others. I think it is quite valuable to work on a new sonnet each day for a couple of weeks. After the initial insecurity even experienced actors feel beginning their work on sonnets, I have found that actors discover a true exhilaration in these gems.

Then go on to soliloquies. You may use those suggested earlier in the book. Or women should try Isabella in *Measure for Measure*, Act II, scene 4:

To whom should I complain? Did I tell this,
Who would believe me? O perilous mouths,
That bear in them one and the self-same tongue
Either of condemnation or approof,
Bidding the law make court'sy to their will,
Hooking both right and wrong to the appetite,
To follow as it draws! I'll to my brother.
Though he hath fallen by prompture of the blood,
Yet hath he in him such a mind of honour,
That, had he twenty heads to tender down
On twenty bloody blocks, he'd yield them up,
Before his sister should her body stoop
To such abhorred pollution.
Then, Isabel, live chaste, and, brother, die:
More than our brother is our chastity.
I'll tell him yet of Angelo's request,
And fit his mind to death, for his soul's rest.

After reading the play and working for at least a week on this soliloquy, begin your work on a scene from the same play: start with Isabella's entrance in *Measure for Measure*, Act II, scene 4, with Angelo.

ANGELO. How now, fair maid!
ISABELLA. I am come to know your pleasure.

Men should try Angelo's soliloquy in *Measure for Measure*, Act II, scene 2:

> *From thee,—even from thy virtue!—*
> *What's this? What's this? Is this her fault or mine?*
> *The tempter or the tempted, who sins most, ha?*
> *Not she; nor doth she tempt; but it is I*
> *That, lying by the violet in the sun,*
> *Do, as the carrion does, not as the flower,*
> *Corrupt with virtuous season. Can it be*
> *That modesty may more betray our sense*
> *Than woman's lightness? Having waste ground enough,*
> *Shall we desire to raze the sanctuary,*
> *And pitch our evils there? O, fie, fie, fie!*
> *What dost thou, or what art thou, Angelo?*
> *Dost thou desire her foully for those things*
> *That make her good? O, let her brother live:*
> *Thieves for their robbery have authority,*
> *When judges steal themselves. What, do I love her,*
> *That I desire to hear her speak again,*
> *And feast upon her eyes? What is't I dream on?*
> *O cunning enemy, that, to catch a saint,*
> *With saints dost bait thy hook! Most dangerous*

Is that temptation that doth goad us on
To sin in loving virtue. Never could the strumpet,
With all her double vigour—art and nature—
Once stir my temper; but this virtuous maid
Subdues me quite. Ever till now
When men were fond, I smiled, and wondered how.

And then try *Measure for Measure*, Act II, scene 4, with Isabella. (Start at the beginning of the scene or at Isabella's entrance.)

Note: When you read the play, do it from beginning to end *out loud,* not just your lines but all the lines. Don't rush your reading. It doesn't matter how long it takes. You will find it getting easier and easier to understand the dialogue and be free with it. You will also find your speech relaxing and becoming less regional. If you do this with a number of his plays, you will never have any trouble acting Shakespeare. It's what I did when I was a student. And it has made Shakespeare's work accessible to me and a joy to read, to act, and to teach.

EPILOGUE

". . . What a piece of work is a man! how noble in reason! how
infinite in faculty! in form and moving how express and admirable!
in action how like an angel! in apprehension how like a god! the
beauty of the world! the paragon of animals!"

—Hamlet in Act II, scene 2

A specific role—especially a great role—requires that the actor prepare in specific ways. An aspiring actor also needs to prepare, in a broader way, for the acting life.

I encourage young actors to go to college—to a liberal arts college, not a conservatory for acting. It is important for young actors to study things that will expand their knowledge and trigger their imaginations, so that they will grow as people and have something to bring to the roles they will eventually play. After college there is plenty of time to go to a conservatory for graduate studies in acting, or for professional training in New York or Los Angeles. But the broader personal studies should continue. Listening to classical music, reading the great novels, poetry, and plays, going to the ballet, and wandering through the great museums broadens your interests, your ear, your eye, your language, taste, and curiosity. It makes you not just a better actor but a complete actor.

I have nothing against rock, rhythm and blues, and other popular forms of music—in fact, I am a lifelong fan of jazz and blues—but I think classical music opens us to sound and feeling in a very different way. It offers a more complex and subtle range of textures, a more elaborate vocabulary. Without the distancing effect of language, it connects directly to our emotions, probing the unconscious and stimulating us profoundly. No wonder research shows that children who are introduced to classical music at an early age display greater concentration, better verbal skills, and higher IQs.

And listening to the music of a given period is crucial preparation for specific roles, like being exposed to the air people breathed in that time and place. If you want to act the characters of Shakespeare, Molière, Chekhov, and Ibsen, you must have John Dowling, Lully, Chopin, Mussorgsky, Schubert, Schumann, and Beethoven in your ear, in your soul. The music will affect how you move, stand, talk, even think. You must be within the sounds of the time in order to embrace the text and freely explore it.

If you are new to classical music, don't stop listening to the music you love. Just add to it. Start with Chopin, because he's so accessibly emotional. Or if you prefer, Bach, Mozart, or Beethoven. Buy a recording. Go to an orchestra concert or a recital. Ask a friend who knows something about classical music to make some recommendations. Better yet, if you can, take a listening appreciation class.

Look at great art—not reproductions but the originals, so that you can see the artist's brush strokes. Instead of connecting you to the period through your ear this will connect you unconsciously through your eyes. As Jennifer Jason Leigh comments, art "moves you in a way that's not cerebral. It can tell you so much about a condition, or about a state, a feeling, a relationship." You don't need to be a scholar to get something out of a piece of art. In fact, small, regular doses are probably best, to keep the imagination from working overtime. When I was a student in New York City, I spent an hour of almost every day roaming the galleries at the Metropolitan Museum of Art. I discovered the monumental power of Rembrandt, the intimacy of Vermeer, Van Gogh, Monet, Renoir, Degas, Manet. It took me six months just to make it through the Impressionists. Little by little the paintings taught me to see faces and expressions, human life, the way these great artists saw it. I still can't stay longer in a museum than about an hour before I start to tire from the images coming at me, visual art is such a powerful stimulus.

Go see classical ballet. It's an acquired taste, and it may take a while for you to appreciate it. But ballet unites music, drama, and movement in a way that is enormously inspiring for an actor's sense of the stage and his movement on it. The drama in ballet is expressed in pure movement. I still rank among the most memorable interpretations of Shakespeare's *Taming of the Shrew* a touring production by the Stuttgart Ballet, choreographed by John Cranko. His view of the story and the characterizations of Kate and Petruchio by dancers Marcia Haydee and Richard Cragen were a revelation to me, and I learned more about Kate's final monologue from the pas de deux at the end of the ballet than I had from a year of touring with the play. In fact it is a love duet between Kate and Petruchio, not a monologue for the actress.

Reading classic novels, poetry, and plays stretches the actor in a different way. It exposes him to language that is richer than our own, and it imparts an understanding of history that period movies, written from a modern sensibility, can't. It also allows him to imagine the landscapes, customs, and manners of a given period. And it can be valuable as inspiration for contemporary characters as well.

When I began work with the brilliant French actor Tcheky Karyo on a Neil Jordan film, *The Good Thief*, he had just been reading the Portuguese poet Fernando Pesoa, who wrote, "Make your reality a dream and your dream a reality." Tcheky had to play a detective in the south of France who is conflicted about his job. Among other complications, he has grown fond of a thief (played by Nick Nolte) who is also a gambler and a drug addict and will spend the rest of his life in jail if he is caught again. On the face of it, the script was a thriller, and the dialogue seemed almost cliché. But Pesoa's poetry had inspired Tcheky with all sorts of ideas and fantasies. He began to see his character as someone who has difficulty with his reality—"Maybe he's quite slow, always bothered by something, forgetting to tie his laces on his shoes, attracted by innocence, sincerity." Tcheky sensed a melancholy in this character and found himself drawing on the music of Mahler. Its spirit of melancholy was mixed with curious flights of lightness and charm. Although the story and character were contemporary, the complexity of the poet's and composer's works played in the actor's ear and heart, bringing out hidden depths.

After all these years, I have not lost my love of art or music or dance or literature. It is much of what I am, and maybe the best part. It's also why Shakespeare, Molière, and Chekhov came so easily to me as an actor. Exposure to great art and artists has given me a broad and deep view of character, and a confidence in my own instinct and imagination. It has inspired me, and it can inspire you, if you give it a chance. It will help you to bring greater depth and imagination to your characters.

So if you want to be an actor, immerse yourself not only in theater but in art, music, dance, and literature. And while you are soaking up art, keep on acting. By all means, pursue the chance to act in whatever medium you can, but always find time to act in plays. I always tell actors, "Make the theater your anchor. Then you will always know who you are." Plays are about character, and on stage there is no place to hide; the audience sees every response, unedited. It's just the actor and the script, and the actor is responsible for everything he says and does. Much as I love film, I still believe that the soul of acting resides in the theater, and it remains the best place for the actor to learn about himself and his acting.

Many colleges have a constant roster of student productions. If those opportunities are available to you, use them. If there is no theater where you are, create one. Put on the great plays—Shakespeare, Chekhov, Strindberg, Ibsen, Molière, Brecht, Beckett, Miller, Williams. Throw yourself into great works so that you have great writers' dialogue to explore. This will take you to explorations of yourself. It doesn't matter whether you succeed in the part or not. You are young. No one expects you to get it right, especially with these plays. But if you fail on good material, you will still learn. And you will not be afraid of these plays later, when you are supposed to know something.

Finally, avoid expending your energy on too much consideration of "the business." Put your concentration on the work of growing as an actor and a human being. Discover what makes you tick as an actor. Use what works and discard whatever gets in the way, no matter how sound the concept. Find your own way, and "the business" will find you.

ACKNOWLEDGMENTS

This book would not have been possible without the help of David Finkle. He encouraged me to write it in my own words so that the reader could hear me directly. He helped me to trust my writing, which was very difficult for me. I thank him for his generosity in sharing himself, not just his expertise and insight, but his warmth and sensitivity. The enormous amount of time we spent together from the very beginning of this project made the book a reality.

My editor, Rebecca Saletan, did something for which I will always be indebted, and for which I cannot thank her enough: she listened to what I said about acting, and she truly "got it." Because of her integrity, the editing was always true to my work. She helped me to clarify a process that seemed impossible to get down on paper. In addition, she made it possible to bridge the gap between the literary and performing worlds with wit, intelligence, and unwavering honesty.

Thank you to my agent, Charlotte Sheedy, whose wisdom and enthusiasm set all the wheels in motion.

My endless gratitude to Kevin Kline, who, in allowing me to talk in depth about our long relationship as teacher and student, continues to astonish me with his courage and determination to take risks. It is this quality, combined with his boundless imagination, that touches all of us who love his acting.

To Brigitte Lacombe, *un bisou* for your incredible artistry, and for making it fun!

My thanks to Ellen Wolf for transcribing my longhand scrawls, and for helping to fill in gaps in the writing from a student's point of view, by allowing me to tape some of our coaching sessions together.

To the actors who provided interviews in which they shared their experiences of working with me, I offer my deepest gratitude. They have made this book a personal journey which I hope will give the reader a more organic understanding of the work I do. Thank you to Kevin Kline, Glenn Close, James Gandolfini, Matt Dillon, Christopher Reeve, Peter Fonda, Bridget Fonda, Ally Sheedy, Jennifer Jason Leigh, Tcheky Karyo, and Chris Noth for giving me the gift of your time, your thoughts, your words.

To the long list of actors I have coached and taught, a special thank you for your trust. Working with you has given me a lifetime of joy.

Most of all, I want to thank my wife, Sandra Jennings, for never taking her hand from mine. It was her idea that I write this book—and her conviction that I could do it if I trusted myself and my instinct, in much the same way as I ask actors to do, when I ask them to reveal themselves in front of an audience and take that thrilling leap of faith to freedom, which is what acting is all about.